PURE

AND

SIMPLE

Upāsikā Kee Nanayon

PURE
AND
SIMPLE

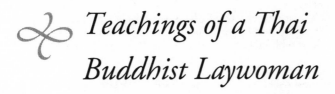 *Teachings of a Thai Buddhist Laywoman*

Upāsikā Kee Nanayon
(K. Khao-suan-luang)

Translated and with an Introduction by
Ṭhānissaro Bhikkhu

 WISDOM PUBLICATIONS • BOSTON

Wisdom Publications
199 Elm Street
Somerville, MA 02144 USA
www.wisdompubs.org

Library of Congress Cataloging-in-Publication Data
Khō. Khaosūanlūang (Kī Khaoūanlūang), 1901-1978.
 [Selections. English. 2005]
 Pure and simple : teachings of a Thai Buddhist laywoman / Upāsikā
Kee Nanayon (K. Khao-suan-luang) ; translated and with an intro-
duction by Thanissaro Bhikkhu.
   p. cm.
 In English, translated from Thai.
 "The passages translated here are taken from Upāsikā Kee's extempo-
raneous talks"—Introd.
 Includes bibliographical references and index.
 ISBN 0-86171-492-X (pbk. : alk. paper)
 1. Meditation—Buddhism. 2. Buddhism—Doctrines. I. Title: Pure
and simple. II. DeGraff, Geoffrey. III. Title.
 BQ5625.K65 2005
 294.3'444—dc22
                                   2004029380
First Edition
09 08 07 06 05
5 4 3 2

Cover design by Suzanne Heiser.

Interior design by Dede Cummings. Set in Centaur Mt 11.5/16.25.

Wisdom Publications' books are printed on acid-free paper and meet the guidelines
 for permanence and durability set by the Committee on Production Guidelines for
Book Longevity of the Council on Library Resources.

Printed in Canada.

CONTENTS

INTRODUCTION

Upāsikā Kee Nanayon, also known by her pen name, K. Khao-suan-luang, was the foremost woman Dhamma teacher in twentieth-century Thailand. Born in 1901 to a Chinese merchant family in Rajburi, a town to the west of Bangkok, she was the eldest of five children—or, counting her father's children by a second wife, the eldest of eight. Her mother was a religious woman and taught her the rudiments of Buddhist practice, such as nightly chants and the observance of the precepts, from an early age. In later life she described how, at the age of six, she became so filled with fear and loathing at the miseries her mother went through during the pregnancy and birth of one of Kee's younger siblings that, on seeing the newborn child for the first time—"sleeping quietly, a little red thing with black, black hair"—she ran away from home for three days. This experience, plus the anguish she must have felt when her parents separated, probably lay behind her decision, made when she was still quite young, never to submit to what she saw as the slavery of marriage.

During her teens she devoted her spare time to Dhamma books and to meditation, and her working hours to running a small store to support her father in his old age. Her meditation progressed well enough that she was able to teach him meditation, with fairly good results, in the last year of his life. After his death she continued her business with the thought of saving up enough money to enable herself to live the remainder of her life in a secluded place and give herself fully to the practice. Her aunt and uncle, who were also interested in Dhamma practice, had a small home near a forested hill, Khao Suan Luang (Royal Park Mountain, the place that inspired her choice of pen name), outside of Rajburi, where she often went to practice. In 1945, as life disrupted by World War II had begun to return to normal, she handed her store over to her younger sister, joined her aunt and uncle in moving to the hill, and there the three of them began a life devoted entirely to meditation, taking on the titles of upāsaka and upāsikā—male and female lay devotees of the Buddha. The small retreat they made for themselves in an abandoned monastic dwelling eventually grew to become the nucleus of a women's practice center that has flourished to this day.

Life at the retreat was frugal, in line with the fact that outside support was minimal in the early years. However, even now that the center has become well known and fully established, the same frugality is maintained for its benefits—subduing greed, pride, and other mental defilements—as well as for the pleasure it offers in unburdening the heart. The women practicing at the center are all vegetarian and abstain from such stimulants as tobacco, coffee, tea, and betel nut. They meet daily for chanting, group meditation, and discussion of the practice. In the years when Upāsikā Kee's health was still strong, she would hold special meetings at which the members would report on their practice, after which she would give a talk touching on important issues they had brought up in their reports. It was during such sessions that most of the talks recorded in this volume were given.

In the center's early years, small groups of friends and relatives would visit on occasion to give support and to listen to Upāsikā Kee's Dhamma talks. As word spread of the high standard of her teachings and practice, larger groups came to visit and more women joined the community. Although many of her students were ordained eight-precept nuns, robed in white, she herself maintained the status of an eight-precept laywoman all her life.

When tape-recording was introduced to Thailand in the mid-1950s, friends began recording her talks, and in 1956 a group of them printed a small volume of her transcribed talks for free distribution. By the mid-1960s, the stream of free Dhamma literature from Khao Suan Luang—Upāsikā Kee's poetry as well as her talks—had grown to a flood. This attracted even more people to her center and established her as one of the best-known Dhamma teachers, male or female, in Thailand.

Upāsikā Kee was something of an autodidact. Although she picked up the rudiments of meditation during her frequent visits to monasteries in her youth, she practiced mostly on her own without any formal study under a meditation teacher. Most of her instruction came from books—the Pali Canon and the works of contemporary teachers—and was tested in the crucible of her own relentless honesty.

In the later years of her life she developed cataracts that eventually resulted in blindness, but she still continued a rigorous schedule of meditating and receiving visitors interested in the Dhamma. She passed away quietly in 1978 after entrusting the center to a committee she appointed from among its members. Her younger sister,

Upāsikā Wan, who up to that point had played a major role as a supporter and facilitator for the center, joined the community within a few months of Upāsikā Kee's death and soon became its leader, a position she held until her own death in 1993. Now the center is once again being run by committee and has grown to accommodate sixty members.

A NOTE ON THE TRANSLATIONS

With two exceptions, the passages translated here are taken from Upāsikā Kee's extemporaneous talks. The first exception is the prologue, excerpted from a poem she wrote on the twentieth anniversary of the founding of the center at Khao Suan Luang, in which she reflects on life at the center in its early years. The second exception is the first piece, "The Practice in Brief," a brief outline of the practice that she wrote as an introduction to one of her early volumes of talks.

With two other exceptions, all of the passages are translated directly from the Thai. Many have previously appeared in books privately printed in Thailand or published by the Buddhist Publication Society in Sri Lanka. One book of her talks—printed under the titles *Directing to Self-Penetration* and *Directions for Insight*—was originally translated by another hand. A long search, conducted by Upāsikā Sumana Hengsawat in the Khao Suan Luang library, succeeded in uncovering the Thai originals for only four of the six talks in that volume, which are here translated in "Going against the Flow." As for the remaining two, I thoroughly revised the existing translations to bring them more in line with Upāsikā

Kee's straightforward, no-nonsense style. Seeing how far the earlier translations of the other four talks diverged from the original Thai, I cannot guarantee the accuracy of the two revised talks. Still, they contain valuable Dhamma lessons and so I have included them as the first two talks in "Going against the Flow." To make that collection more complete, I have added another talk—"Stop, Look, and Let Go"—translated directly from the Thai.

My aim in translation has been to adhere as closely as possible to the Thai both in substance and in style. This has meant including a fair amount of repetition, but I have found that the repetition plays a large role in the forcefulness of Upāsikā Kee's presentation and feel no qualms about leaving it in. The talks work especially well if read aloud.

Ṭhānissaro Bhikkhu
METTA FOREST MONASTERY
VALLEY CENTER, CALIFORNIA

PROLOGUE

In 1965, soon after the death of her uncle, Upāsikā Kee wrote a long poem on the first twenty years at Khao Suan Luang. What follows is a prose paraphrase of some of its passages.

On June 26, 1945, the three of us—my aunt, uncle, and myself—first came to stay in the old meeting hall on Khao Suan Luang. Uncle Plien Raksae handled the repairs. He used to be a farmer living on the other side of the hill, but he had left the worries of home to practice the Dhamma.

The place was an old monastic retreat that several monks had set up and then abandoned many years before. Next to the meeting hall was an octagonal cement tank for collecting rainwater from the roof of the hall—enough to last all year. Old meditation huts at distant intervals lined the path up the hill to the hall. Local laypeople had dug a large pond at the foot of the hill to collect rainwater, but it would dry up in the hot season. An old oxcart track at the edge of the pond circled the hill, marking off an area of thirty acres where we decided to make our retreat.

When we first arrived, the place was overgrown with bushes and weeds, so we had to clear paths through the forest and up the hill to the cave under the cliff face—a cave we called Uttama Santi, Highest Peace Cave. It was much fun, clearing the forest day after day, and soon another woman joined us. In those days there were no visitors, so the place was very quiet.

When I first came I was afraid of ghosts and of people, but my resolve was firm, and my belief in *kamma* gradually lessened my worries and fears. I had never before lived in the forest. I hadn't seen any purpose in it before, and I thought that it would be better to stay in the town, running a store and making enough money to last me the rest of my life. But coming to the forest and living very simply, I came to feel lighthearted and free. Seeing nature all around me inspired me to explore inside my own mind.

> With no struggling, no thinking,
> the mind, still,
> will see cause and effect
> vanishing in the Void.
> Attached to nothing, letting go:
> Know that this is the way
> to allay all stress.

For food, we lived off the delicious bamboo shoots growing in the bamboo clusters at the top of the hill. The bitter fruits and berries that the trees produced during the rainy season provided our medicine. As for utensils, we used whatever we could find in the forest. Coconut shells, for instance, made excellent bowls: You didn't have to worry about their getting broken. We kept patching our old clothes and slept on old mats and wooden pillows in the meeting hall. Up in the cave I kept another wooden pillow to use when I rested. Wooden pillows are ideal for meditators. If you use soft ones, you have to worry about putting them away safely.

All sorts of animals lived around the hill: wildcats, wildfowl, rabbits, moles, lizards, snakes. Bands of monkeys would pester us from time to time when they came to eat the fruit off the trees. The calls of owls and mourning doves filled the air. Throngs of bats lived in the cave, flying out at night and returning just before dawn. As for the ants and termites, they couldn't fly, so they walked, always so intent—on going where? And what were they carrying with such active cooperation?

Coming here, we cut off all memories of the past and thought only of making progress in our search for release from suffering. Visitors came and went. More people came to stay with us, intent on learning strategies for training the mind, and their burdens of suffering would lessen. Never trained to teach, I now often found myself discussing the practice and skillful means for contemplating the five aggregates. All those who came to practice had frequented monasteries before, so they were already well educated in the Dhamma and approached the practice in a clear-eyed manner. We met frequently to discuss the many techniques to use in training the heart to explore the body and mind skillfully.

Now, after twenty years, the forest is no longer wild, and the place has been improved in numerous ways to make it more conducive to the practice for going beyond the cycle of suffering and stress. If we continue progressing in the path, following the example of the Noble Disciples—with sincerity, truth, and endurance in our efforts to explore the five aggregates intelligently—we are sure to see the results we hope for.

> Please help keep this forest fragrant
> till earth and sky are no more,
> the forest of Royal Park Mountain,
> still garden of calm
> where the Dhamma resounds:
> > the Unbound—nibbāna—
> > is a nature devoid
> > of all suffering.

LOOKING INWARD

THE PRACTICE IN BRIEF

This training, which is easy to learn, gives immediate results, and is suitable for every time and place, and for people of every age and either sex, is to study in the school of this body—a fathom long, a cubit wide, and a span thick—with its perceiving mind in charge. This body has many things, ranging from the crude to the subtle, that are well worth knowing.

Those who practice the Dhamma should train themselves to understand in the following stages:

First, know that the body is composed of various physical properties, the major ones being the properties of earth, water, fire, and wind; the minor ones being the aspects that adhere to the major ones: things like color, smell, shape.

These properties are inconstant, stressful, and unclean. If you look into them deeply, you will see that there's no substance to them at all. They are simply impersonal conditions, with nothing worth calling "me" or "mine." When you can clearly perceive the body in these terms, you will be able to let go of any clinging or attachment to it as an entity, your self, someone else, this or that.

Second, deal with mental phenomena (feelings, perceptions, thought-fabrications, and consciousness). Focus on keeping track of the truth that these are characterized by arising, persisting, and then disbanding. In other words, their nature is to arise and disband, arise and disband repeatedly. When you see this truth, you will be able to let go of your attachments to mental phenomena as entities—as your self, someone else, this or that.

Third, training on the level of practice doesn't simply mean studying, listening, or reading. You have to practice so as to see clearly with your own mind in the following steps:

Start out by brushing aside all external concerns and turn to look inside at your own mind until you know in what ways it is clear or murky, calm or unsettled. To do this, put mindfulness and alertness in charge as you keep aware of the body and mind until you've trained the mind to stay firmly in a state of normalcy or neutrality.

Once the mind can stay in a state of normalcy, you'll see mental fabrications and preoccupations in their natural state of arising and disbanding. The mind will be empty, neutral, and still—neither pleased nor displeased—and will see physical and mental phenomena as they arise and disband naturally, of their own accord.

When the knowledge that there is no self to any of these things becomes thoroughly clear, you will meet with something that lies further inside, beyond all suffering and stress, free from the cycles of change—deathless—free from birth as well as death, for all things that take birth must by nature age, grow ill, and die.

When you see this truth clearly, the mind will be empty, not holding on to anything. It won't even assume itself to be a mind or anything at all. In other words, it won't latch onto itself as being anything of any sort. All that will remain is a pure condition of Dhamma.

Those who see this pure condition of Dhamma in full clarity are bound to grow disenchanted with the repeated sufferings of life. When they thoroughly know the truth of the world and the Dhamma, they will see clearly, right in the present, *that there is something that lies beyond all suffering.* They will know this without having to ask or take it on faith from anyone, for the Dhamma is *paccattaṁ*—something really to be known for oneself. Those who have seen this truth within themselves will attest to it always.

AN HOUR'S MEDITATION

For those of you who have never sat in meditation, here is how it's done: Fold your legs, one on top of the other, but don't cut off the nerves or the blood flow, or else the breath energy in your legs will stagnate and cause you pain. Sit straight and place your hands one on top of the other on your lap. Hold your head up straight and keep your back straight—as if you had a yardstick running along your spine. You have to work at keeping it straight, you know. Don't spend the time slouching and then stretching up again, or the mind won't be able to settle down and be still.

Keep the body straight and your mindfulness firm—firmly with the breath. However coarse or refined your breath may be, simply breathe in naturally. You don't have to force the breath or tense your body. Simply breathe in and out in a relaxed way. Only then will the mind begin to settle down. As soon as the breath grows refined in a natural way and the mind has begun to settle down, focus your attention on the mind itself. If it slips off elsewhere, or thoughts intrude, simply keep your awareness focused right at the mind. Know the mind right at the mind with every in-and-out breath for the entire hour.

In treating the breath as a leash to tie the mind in place so that it doesn't go wandering off, you have to use your endurance. That is, you have to endure pain. For example, when you sit for a long time there's going to be pain because you've never sat for so long before. So first make sure that you keep the mind normal and neutral. When pain arises, don't focus on it. Let go of it as much as you can. Let go of it and focus on your mind. For those of you who've never done this before, it may take a while. Whenever any pain or anything arises, if the mind is affected by craving or defilement, it'll struggle because it doesn't want pain. All it wants is pleasure.

This is where you have to be patient and endure the pain *because pain is something that has to occur.* If there's pleasure, don't get enthralled with it. If there's pain, don't push it away. Start out by keeping the mind neutral. That is your basic stance. Then whenever pleasure or pain arises, don't get pleased or upset. Keep the mind continuously neutral and figure out how to let go. If there's a lot of pain, you first have to endure it and then relax your attachments. Don't think of the pain as being *your* pain. Let it be the pain of the body, the pain of nature.

If the mind latches tight onto anything, it really suffers. It struggles. So here we patiently endure and let go. You have to practice so that you're really good at handling pain. If you can let go of physical pain, you'll be able to let go of other sorts of suffering and pain as well. Keep watching the pain, knowing it, and letting it go. Once you can let it go, you don't need a lot of endurance. It takes a lot of endurance only at the beginning. Once the pain arises, separate the mind from it. Let it be the pain of the body. Don't let the mind be pained too.

This is something that requires equanimity. If you can maintain equanimity in the face of pleasure or pain, it can make the mind peaceful—even though the pain is still pain. The mind keeps knowing, enduring the pain so as to let it go.

After you've worked at this a good while, you'll come to see how important the ways of the mind are. The mind may be hard to train, but keep training it. If you have the time, you can practice at home, at night or early in the morning. Keeping watch over your mind, you'll gain the understanding that comes from mindfulness and discernment. Those who don't train like this go through life— birth, aging, illness, and death—not knowing anything at all about the mind.

If you know your own mind, then when any really heavy illness comes along, your awareness of the mind will help lessen the pain. But this is something you have to work at. It's not easy, yet once the mind is well trained, there's no match for it. It can do away with pain and suffering and doesn't get restless and agitated. It's still and cool—refreshed and blooming right there within itself. So try to experience this still, quiet mind.

This is a really important skill to develop, because it will weaken craving, defilement, and attachment. All of us have defilements, you know. Greed, anger, and delusion cloud our hearts. If we haven't trained ourselves in meditation, our hearts are constantly burning with suffering and stress. Even the pleasure we feel over external things is pleasure only in half measures, because there's suffering and stress in the delusion that thinks these things are pleasurable. As for the pleasure that comes from the practice, it's a cool pleasure that lets go of everything, really free from any sense of me or mine. I ask that you reach the Dhamma that's the real meat inside this aspect of awareness undisturbed by defilement, undisturbed by pain or anything else.

Even though there's pain in the body, you have to figure out how to let it go. The body is simply the four elements—earth, water, wind, and fire. It keeps showing its inconstancy and stressfulness, so keep your mindfulness neutral, at equanimity. Let the mind be above its feelings—above pleasure, above pain, above everything....

All it really takes is endurance—endurance and relinquishment, letting things go, seeing that they're not us, not ours. This is a point you have to hammer at, over and over. When I say you have to endure, I mean you *really* have to endure. Don't be willing to surrender. Craving is going to keep coming up and whispering—telling you to change things, to go after this pleasure or that—but don't listen to it. You have to listen to the Buddha, who tells you to let go of craving. Otherwise, craving will plaster and paint things over; the mind will struggle and won't be able to settle down. So you have to give it your all. Look at this hour as a special hour—special in that you're using special endurance *to keep watch on your own heart and mind.*

A BASIC ORDER IN LIFE

The most important thing in the daily life of a person who practices the Dhamma is to keep to the precepts and to care for them more than you care for your life—to maintain them in a way that the Noble Ones would praise. If you don't have this sort of regard for the precepts, then the vices that run counter to them will become your everyday habits.

Meditators who see that the breaking of a precept is something trifling and insignificant spoil their entire practice. If you can't practice even these basic, beginning levels of the Dhamma, it will ruin all the qualities you'll be trying to develop in the later stages of the practice. This is why you have to stick to the precepts as your basic foundation and to keep a lookout for anything in your behavior that falls short of them. Only then will you be able to benefit from your practice for the sake of eliminating your sufferings with greater and greater precision.

If you simply act in line with the cravings and desires swelling out of a sense of self that doesn't fear the fires of defilement, you'll have to suffer both in this life and in lives to come. If you don't have a sense of conscience—a sense of shame at the thought of doing shoddy actions, and a fear of their consequences—your practice will deteriorate day by day.

When people live without any order to their lives—without even the basic order that comes with the precepts—there's no way they can attain purity. We have to examine ourselves: In what ways at present are we breaking our precepts in thought, word, or deed? If we simply let things pass and aren't intent on examining ourselves to see the harm that comes from breaking the precepts and following the defilements, our practice can only sink lower and lower. Instead of extinguishing defilements and suffering, it will simply succumb to the power of craving. If this is the case, what damage is done? How much freedom does the mind lose? These are things we have to learn for ourselves. When we do, our practice of self-inspection in higher matters will get solid results and won't go straying off into nonsense. For this reason, whenever craving or defilement shows itself in our actions, we have to catch hold of it and examine what's going on inside the mind.

Once we're aware with real mindfulness and discernment, we'll see the poison and power of the defilements. We'll feel disgust for them and want to extinguish them as much as we can. But if we use our defilements to examine things, they'll say everything is fine. The same as when we're predisposed to liking someone. Even if he does something wrong, we say he's right. This is the way the defilements are. They say that everything we do is right and throw all the blame on other people, other things. So we can't trust it—this sense of "self" in which craving and defilement lord it over the heart. We can't trust it at all.

The violence of defilement, or this sense of self, is like that of a fire burning a forest or a house. It won't listen to anyone but simply keeps burning away, burning away inside of you. And that's not all. It's always out to set fire to other people too.

The fires of suffering, of defilement, consume all those who don't contemplate themselves or who don't have any means of putting them out. People of this sort can't withstand the power of the defilements, can't help but follow along wherever their cravings lead. The moment they're provoked, they follow in line with these things. This is why the sensations in the mind when provoked by defilement are very important, for they can lead you to do things with no sense of shame, no fear for the consequences of doing evil—which means that you're sure to break your precepts.

Once you've followed the defilements, they feel really satisfied—like arsonists who feel gleeful when they've set other people's places on fire. As soon as you've called somebody something vile or spread some malicious gossip, the defilements really like it. Your sense of self really likes it, because acting in line with defilements like that gives it real satisfaction. As a consequence, it keeps filling itself with vices that run counter to the precepts, falling into hell in this very lifetime without realizing it. So take a good look at the violence the defilements do to you, to see whether you should keep socializing with them, whether you should regard them as your friends or your enemies.

As soon as any wrong views or ideas come out of the mind, we have to analyze them and turn around so as to catch sight of the facts within us. No matter what issues the defilements raise, always focusing on the faults of others, we have to turn around and look within. *When we realize our own faults and can come to our senses—* that's where our study of the Dhamma, our practice of the Dhamma, shows its real rewards.

CONTINUOUS PRACTICE

The passage for reflection on the four requisites (clothing, food, shelter, and medicine) is a fine pattern for contemplation, but we never actually get down to putting it to use. We're taught to memorize it, not simply to pass the time of day or so that we can talk about it every now and then, but so that we will contemplate the requisites and really know them with our own mindfulness and discernment. If we actually get down to contemplating in line with the established pattern, our minds will become much less influenced by unwise thoughts. But it's the rare person who genuinely makes this a continuous practice. For the most part we're not interested. We don't feel like contemplating this sort of thing. We'd much rather contemplate whether this or that food will taste good or not, and if it doesn't taste good, how to fix it so that it will. That's the sort of thing we like to contemplate.

Try to see the filthiness of food and of the physical properties in general, to see their emptiness of any real entity or self. There's nothing of any substance to the physical properties of the body, which are all rotten and decomposing. The body is like a rest room over a cesspool. We can decorate it on the outside to make it pretty and attractive, but on the inside it's full of the most horrible, filthy things. Whenever we excrete anything, we ourselves are repelled by it; yet even though we're repelled by it, it's there inside us, in our intestines—decomposing, full of worms, awful smelling. There's just the flimsiest membrane covering it up, yet we fall for it and hold tight to it. We don't see the constant decomposition of this body, in spite of the filth and smells it sends out.

The reason we're taught to memorize the passage for reflecting on the requisites, and to use it for contemplation, is so that we'll see the inconstancy of the body. We see that there's no "self" to any of it or to any of the mental phenomena we sense at every moment.

We contemplate mental phenomena to see clearly that they're not-self, to see this with every moment. The moments of the mind—the arising, persisting, and disbanding of mental sensations—are very subtle and fast. To see them, the mind has to be quiet. If the mind is involved in distractions, thoughts, and imaginings, we won't be able to penetrate it. We won't see its characteristics as it deals with its objects, or what the arising and disbanding within it is like.

This is why we have to practice concentration: to make the mind quiet, to provide a foundation for our contemplation. For instance, you can focus on the breath, or be aware of the mind as it focuses on the breath. Actually, when you focus on the breath, you're also aware of the mind. And again, the mind is what knows the breath. So you focus exclusively on the breath together with the mind. Don't think of anything else, and the mind will settle down and grow still. Once it attains stillness on this level, that's the time to contemplate.

Making the mind still so that you can contemplate it is something you have to keep working at in the beginning. The same holds true with training yourself to be mindful and fully alert in all your activities. You really have to work at this continuously, doing it all the time. At the same time, you have to arrange the external conditions of your life so that you won't have any concerns to distract you.

Now, of course, the practice is something you can do in any set of circumstances—for example, when you come home from work you can sit and meditate for a while—but when you're trying seriously to make it continuous, to make it habitual, it's much more difficult. "Making it habitual" means being fully mindful and alert with each in-and-out breath, wherever you go, whatever you do, whether you're healthy, sick, or whatever, and regardless of what happens inside or out. *The mind has to be in a state of all-encompassing awareness while keeping track of the arising and disbanding of mental phenomena at all times*—to the point where you can stop the mind from forming thoughts under the power of craving and defilement the way it used to before you began the practice.

EVERY IN-AND-OUT BREATH

Try keeping your awareness with the breath to see what the still mind is like. It's very simple, all the rules have been laid out, but when you actually try to do it, something resists. It's hard. But when you let your mind think 108 or 1,009 things about no matter what, you find it very easy, not hard at all. *Try and see if you can engage your mind with the breath in the same way it's been engaged with the defilements.* Try engaging it with the breath and see what happens. See if you can disperse the defilements with every in-and-out breath. Why is it that the mind can stay engaged with the defilements all day long and yet go for entire days without knowing how heavy or subtle the breath is at all?

So try and be observant. The bright, clear awareness that can stem from staying focused constantly on the mind: Sometimes a strong sensory contact comes along and makes it blur and fade away with no trouble at all. But if you can keep hold of the breath as a reference point, that state of mind becomes more stable and sure, more secure. It has two fences around it: mindfulness coupled with the breath. If there's only one fence, it can easily break.

TAKING A STANCE

Normally the mind isn't willing to stop and look, to stop and know itself, which is why we have to keep training it continually so that it will settle down from its restlessness and grow still. Let your desires and thought processes settle down. Let the mind take its stance in a state of normalcy, not liking or disliking anything. To reach a basic level of emptiness and freedom, you first have to take a stance. If you don't have a stance against which to measure things, progress will be very difficult. If your practice is hit or miss—a bit of this, a little of that—you won't get any results. So the mind first has to take a stance.

When you take a stance that the mind can maintain in a state of normalcy, don't go slipping off into the future. Have the mind know itself in the stance of the present: "Right now it's in a state of normalcy. No likes or dislikes have arisen yet. It hasn't created any issues. It's not being disturbed by a desire for this or that."

Then look into the basic level of the mind to see if it's as normal and empty. If you're really looking inside, really aware inside, then *that which is looking and knowing is mindfulness and discernment in and of itself.* You don't need to search for anything anywhere else to come and do your looking for you. As soon as you stop to see whether the mind is in a state of normalcy, then if it's normal, you'll know immediately that it's normal. If it's not, you'll know immediately that it's not.

Take care to keep this awareness going. If you can keep knowing like this continuously, the mind will be able to keep its stance continuously as well. As soon as the thought occurs to you to check things out, you'll immediately stop and look, without any need to go searching for knowledge anywhere else. You look, you know, right there at the mind, and you can tell whether or not it's empty and still. Once you see that it is, then you investigate to see *how* it's empty, *how* it's still. It's not the case that once it's empty and still, that's the end of the matter. *That's not the case at all.* You have to keep watch; you have to investigate at all times. Only then will you see the changing—the arising and disbanding—occurring in that emptiness, that stillness, that state of normalcy.

THE DETAILS OF PAIN

Keeping constant supervision over the mind is a way of learning what life is for. It's a way of learning how we can act so as to rid ourselves of suffering and stress—because the suffering caused by defilement, attachment, and craving is sure to take many different forms. If we don't understand suffering and stress through mindfulness and discernment, we'll live obliviously, going wherever events lead us.

Mindfulness and discernment are tools for knowing ourselves, for testing ourselves so that we won't be careless or complacent, oblivious to the fact that suffering is basically what life is all about.

This point is something we really have to comprehend so that we can live without being oblivious. The pains and discontent that fill our bodies and minds all show us the truths of inconstancy, stress, and not-selfness within us. If you contemplate what's going on inside, right down to the details, you'll see the truths that appear within and without, all of which come down to inconstancy, stress, and not-selfness. But the delusion that's basic to our nature will see everything wrong—as constant, easeful, and self—and so make us live obliviously, even though there's nothing to guarantee how long our lives will last.

Our dreams and delusions make us forget that we live in the midst of a mass of pain and stress—the stress of defilements, the pain of birth. Birth, aging, illness, and death: All are painful and stressful in the midst of instability and change. They're things we have no control over, for they circle around in line with the laws of *kamma* and the defilements we've been amassing all along. Life that floats along in the round of rebirth is thus nothing but stress and pain.

If we can find a way to develop our mindfulness and discernment, we'll cut the round of rebirth so that we won't have to keep wandering on. Mindfulness and discernment will help us know that birth is painful, aging is painful, illness is painful, death is painful, and that these are all things that defilement, attachment, and craving keep driving through the cycles of change.

So as long as we have the opportunity, we should study the truths that appear within our body and mind. Then we'll come to know that the elimination of stress and pain, the elimination of defilement, is a function of our practice of the Dhamma. If we don't practice the Dhamma, we'll keep floating along in the round of rebirth that's so drearily repetitious—repetitious in its birth, aging, illness, and death, driven on by defilement, attachment, and craving, causing us repeated stress, repeated pain. Living beings for the most part don't know where their stress and pain come from, because they've never studied them, never contemplated them, so they stay stupid and deluded, wandering on and on without end.

If we can stop and be still, the mind will have a chance to be free, to contemplate its suffering, and to let go. This will give the mind a measure of peace because it will no longer want anything from the round of rebirth—for it sees that there's nothing lasting in it, that it's simply stress over and over again. Whatever you grab hold of is stress. This is why you need mindfulness and discernment, so that you can supervise the mind and keep it calm, without letting it fall victim to temptation.

This practice is of the highest importance. People who don't study or practice the Dhamma have wasted their birth as human beings: They're born deluded and simply *stay* deluded. But if we study the Dhamma, we'll become wise to suffering and know the path of practice for freeing ourselves.

Once we follow the right path, the defilements won't be able to drag us around and burn us, because *we* have started to burn *them* away. We come to realize that the more we can burn them away, the more strength of mind we gain. If we let the defilements burn us, the mind will be sapped of its strength, which is why this is something you have to be very careful about. Keep burning away the defilements in every activity, and your mindfulness and discernment will grow stronger and deal bravely with all sorts of suffering and pain.

You must come to see the world as nothing but stress. There's no real ease to it at all. The awareness we gain from mindfulness and discernment will make us disenchanted with life in the world because it will see things for what they are, both within us and without.

The entire world is nothing but an affair of delusion, an affair of suffering. People who don't know the Dhamma, don't practice the Dhamma—no matter what their status or position in life—lead deluded, oblivious lives. When they fall ill or are about to die, they're bound to suffer enormously because they haven't taken the time to understand the defilements that burn their hearts and minds in everyday life. If we make a constant practice of studying and contemplating ourselves—if we make this our everyday activity—it'll help free us from all sorts of suffering and distress. And when we see this, how can we *not* want to practice?

Only intelligent people, though, will be able to stick with the practice. Foolish people won't want to bother. They'd much rather follow the defilements than burn them away. To practice the Dhamma you need a certain basic level of intelligence—enough to have seen at least something of the stress and suffering that come from defilement. Only then can your practice progress. And no matter how difficult it gets, you'll have to keep practicing on to the end.

This practice isn't something you do from time to time, you know. You have to keep at it continuously throughout life. Even if it involves so much physical pain or mental anguish that tears are bathing your cheeks, you have to keep with the holy life because you're playing for real. If you don't follow the holy life, you'll get trapped in suffering and flames. So you have to learn your lessons from pain. Try to contemplate it until you can understand it and let it go, and you'll gain one of life's greatest rewards.

Don't think that you were born to gain this or that level of comfort. You were born to study pain and the causes of pain, and to follow the practice that frees you from pain. This is the most important thing there is. Everything else is trivial and unimportant. All that's important lies with the practice.

Don't think that the defilements will go away easily. When they don't come in blatant forms, they come in subtle ones—and the dangers of the subtle ones are hard to see. Your contemplation will have to be subtle, too, if you want to get rid of them. You'll come to realize that this practice of the Dhamma, in which we contemplate to get to the details inside us, is like sharpening our tools so that, when stress and suffering arise, we can weaken them and cut them away. If your mindfulness and discernment are resolute, the defilements will lose out to them. But if you don't train your mindfulness and discernment to be resolute, the defilements will crush you to pieces.

We were born to do battle with the defilements and to strengthen our mindfulness and discernment. The worth of our practice will increase if, in our everyday life, we do continuous battle with the stresses and pains caused by defilement, craving, and temptation— for then the defilements will grow thin while our mindfulness and discernment grow strong. We'll sense that the mind isn't as troubled and restless as it used to be. It's grown peaceful and calm. The stress of defilement, attachment, and craving has grown weaker. Even though we haven't yet wiped these things out completely, they've grown continually weaker because we haven't fed them. We haven't given them shelter. And we continue to do what we can to weaken them so that they grow thinner all the time.

We have to be fearless in contemplating stress and pain, because when we don't feel much suffering we tend to get complacent. But when the pain and suffering in our body and mind grow sharp and biting, we have to use our mindfulness and discernment to be strong. *Don't let your spirits be weak.* Only then will you be able to do away with your suffering and pain.

We have to learn our lessons from pain so that ultimately the mind becomes free of it, instead of always being weak and losing out to it. We have to be brave in doing battle with it to the ultimate point—when we reach the stage where we can let it go. Pain is always present in this conglomerate of body and mind. It's here for us to see with every moment. If we contemplate it till we know all its details, we can then make it our sport to see pain as a natural condition and not *our* pain. This is something we have to research so as to get to the details: *that it's not our pain,* it's the pain of the aggregates [form, feeling, perception, thought-fabrications, and consciousness]. Knowing in this way means that we can separate out the properties of physical form and mind—to see how they interact, how they change. It's really fascinating.... Watching pain builds up lots of mindfulness and discernment.

But if you focus on pleasure and ease, you'll simply stay deluded like people in general. They get carried away by the pleasure that comes from watching or listening to things they like—but then when pain comes and tears run down their cheeks, think of how much they suffer! And then they have to be parted from their loved ones, which makes it even worse. But those of us who practice the Dhamma don't need to be deluded like that, because we see with every moment that nothing but stress arises, persists, and passes away. Aside from stress, nothing arises; aside from stress, nothing passes away. Stress is there for us to perceive with every moment. If we contemplate it, we'll see it.

So we can't let ourselves be oblivious. This is what the truth is, and we have to study it so as to know it—especially while we are practicing. We have to contemplate stress all the time to see its every manifestation. The arahants live without being oblivious because they know the truth at all times, and their hearts are clean and pure. As for us with our defilements, we have to keep trying, because if we continually supervise our mind with mindfulness and discernment, we'll be able to keep the defilements from making a mess and obscuring it. Even if it does become obscured somehow, we'll be able to remove that obscurity and make the mind empty and free.

This is the practice that weakens all the defilements, attachments, and cravings within us. It's through this practice of the Dhamma that our lives become free. So I ask you to keep working at the practice without being complacent. If in whatever span of life you have left, you keep trying to the full extent of your abilities, you'll gain the mindfulness and discernment to see the facts within yourself, and you'll be able to let go—free from any sense of self, free from any sense of self—continuously.

AWARE RIGHT AT AWARENESS

The mind, if mindfulness and awareness are watching over it, won't meet with any suffering as the result of its actions. If suffering *does* arise, we'll be immediately aware of it and can put it out. This is one point of the practice we can work at constantly. And we can test ourselves by seeing how refined and subtle our all-around awareness is. Whenever the mind slips away and goes out to receive external sensory contact, can it maintain its basic stance of mindfulness or internal awareness? The practice we need to work at in our everyday life is to have constant mindfulness, constant all-around present awareness. Work at it in every posture: sitting, standing, walking, and lying down. Make sure that your mindfulness stays continuous.

Living in this world—the mental and physical phenomena of these five aggregates—gives us plenty to contemplate. We must try to watch them, contemplate them, so that we can understand them—because the truths that we must learn to read in this body and mind are here in every moment. We don't have to get wrapped up in extraneous themes. All the themes we need are right here in the body and mind. As long as we can keep the mind constantly aware all around, we can contemplate them.

If you contemplate mental and physical events and see how they arise and disband right in the here and now, and if you don't get involved with external things—like sights making contact with the eyes, or sounds with the ears—then there really aren't a lot of issues. The mind can be at normalcy, at equilibrium—calm and undisturbed by defilement or the stress of sensory contact. It can look after itself and maintain its balance. You'll come to sense that if you're aware right at awareness itself, without getting involved in external things like mental labels and thoughts, the mind will see how things constantly arise and disband—and won't be embroiled in anything. It'll be disengaged, empty, and free. But if it goes out to label things as good or evil, as "me" or "mine," or gets attached to anything, it'll become unsettled and disturbed.

You have to know that if the mind can be still, totally and presently aware, and capable of contemplating with every activity, then blatant forms of suffering and stress will dissolve away. Even if they start to form, you can be alert to them and disperse them immediately. Once you see this actually happening—even in only the beginning stages—it can disperse a lot of the confusion and turmoil in your heart. In other words, don't let yourself dwell on the past or latch onto thoughts of the future. As for the events arising and passing away in the present, leave them alone. Whatever your duties are, simply perform them as you have to, and the mind won't get worked up. It will, to some extent, become empty and still.

This is something you have to be careful about. You have to see for yourself that *if your mindfulness and discernment are constantly in charge, the truths of the arising and disbanding of mental and physical phenomena are always there for you to see,* always there for you to know. If you look at the body, you'll see it simply as physical properties. If you look at feelings, you'll see them as changing and inconstant: as pleasure, as pain, or as neither pleasure nor pain. To see these things is to see the truth within yourself. Don't let yourself get caught up with your external duties. Simply keep watch. If your awareness is the sort that lets you read yourself correctly, the mind will be able to stay at normalcy, at equilibrium, at stillness, without any resistance.

If the mind can stay with itself and not go out looking for things to criticize or latch onto, it can maintain a natural form of stillness. So this is something we have to try for in our every activity. Keep your conversations to a minimum, and there won't be a whole lot of issues. Keep watch right at the mind. When you keep watch with continuous mindfulness, your senses stay restrained.

Being mindful in this way is something you have to work at. Try it and see. Can you keep this sort of awareness continuous? What sort of things can still get the mind engaged? What sorts of thoughts and labels of good and bad, me and mine, does it think up? Then look to see if these things arise and disband.

The sensations that arise from external contact and internal contact all have the same sorts of characteristics. You have to keep looking until you see this. If you know how to look, you'll see it—and the mind will grow calm.

So the point we have to practice in this more advanced state doesn't have a whole lot of issues. There's nothing you have to do, nothing you have to label, nothing you have to think a whole lot about. Simply look carefully and contemplate, and in this very lifetime you'll have a chance to be calm and at peace, to know yourself profoundly. You'll come to see that the Dhamma is amazing *right here in your own heart.* Don't go searching for the Dhamma outside, for it lies within. Peace lies within, but we have to contemplate so that we're aware all around—subtly, deep down. If you look just on the surface, you won't understand anything. Even if the mind is at normalcy on the ordinary, everyday level, you won't understand much of anything at all.

You have to contemplate so that you're aware all around in a skillful way. The word "skillful" is something you can't explain with words, but you can know for yourself when you see the way in which awareness within the heart becomes special, when you see what this special awareness is about. This is something you can know for yourself.

And there's not really much to it: simply arising, persisting, disbanding. Keep looking until this becomes plain—really, really plain—and everything disappears. All suppositions, all conventional formulations, all those aggregates and properties get swept away, leaving nothing but awareness pure and simple, not involved with anything at all—and there's nothing you have to do to it. Simply stay still and watch, be aware, letting go with every moment.

Simply watching this one thing is enough to do away with all sorts of defilements, all sorts of suffering and stress. If you don't know how to watch it, the mind is sure to get disturbed. It's sure to label things and concoct thoughts. As soon as there's contact at the senses, it'll go looking for things to latch onto, liking and disliking the objects it meets in the present and then getting involved with the past and future, spinning a web to entangle itself.

If you truly look at each moment in the present, there's really nothing at all. You'll see with every mental moment that things disband, disband, disband—really nothing at all. The important point is that you don't go forming issues out of nothing. The physical elements perform their duties in line with their elementary physical nature. The mental elements keep sensing in line with their own affairs. But our stupidity goes looking for issues to cook up, to label, to think about. It goes looking for things to latch onto, and then the mind gets into a turmoil. This point is really all we have to see, the only problem we have to solve. If things are left to their nature pure and simple, there's no "us," no "them." This is a singular truth that will arise for us to know and see. There's nothing else we can know or see that can match it in any way. Once you know and see this one thing, it extinguishes all suffering and stress. The mind will be empty and free, giving no meaning and forming no attachment to anything at all.

This is why looking inward is so special. Whatever arises, simply stop and look at it. Don't get excited by it. If you become excited when any special intuitions arise, you'll get the mind worked up into a turmoil. If you become afraid that this or that will happen, that too will get you in a turmoil. So you have to stop and look, stop and know. The first thing is simply to look, to know. And don't latch onto what you know—because whatever it is, it's simply a phenomenon that arises and disbands, arises and disbands, changing as part of its nature.

So your awareness has to take a firm stance right at the mind in and of itself. In the beginning stages, you have to know that when mindfulness is standing firm, the mind won't be affected by the objects of sensory contact. Keep working at maintaining this stance, holding firm to it. If you gain a sense of this for yourself, really knowing and seeing for yourself, your mindfulness will become even more firm. If anything arises in any way at all, you'll be able to let it go—and all the many troubles and turmoils of the mind will dissolve away.

If mindfulness slips and the mind goes out giving meanings to things, latching onto things, troubles will arise. So you have to keep checking on this in every moment. There's nothing else that's so worth checking on. You have to keep checking on the mind in and of itself, contemplating the mind in and of itself. Or else you can contemplate the body, feelings, or the phenomenon of arising and disbanding—the Dhamma—in and of itself. All of these things are themes you can keep track of entirely within yourself. You don't have to keep track of a lot of themes, because having a lot of themes will make you restless and distracted. First you'll practice this theme, then you'll practice that one, then you'll make comparisons, all of which will keep the mind from growing still.

If you can take your stance at awareness, if you're skilled at looking, the mind can be at peace. You'll know how things arise and disband. First practice keeping awareness right within yourself, so that your mindfulness stays firm, unaffected by the objects of sensory contact, and doesn't label things as good or bad, pleasing or displeasing. You have to keep checking to see that when the mind can be at normalcy, centered and neutral as its primary stance, then—whatever it knows or sees—it will be able to contemplate and let go.

The sensations in the mind that we explain at such length are on the level of labels. Only when there is awareness right at awareness will you really know that the mind that's aware of awareness doesn't send its knowing outside this awareness. There are no issues. Nothing can be concocted in the mind when it knows in this way. In other words,

> An inward-staying
>> unentangled knowing,
> All outward-going knowing
>> cast aside.

The only thing you have to work at maintaining is the state of mind at normalcy—knowing, seeing, and staying in the present. If you don't maintain it, if you don't keep looking after it, then when sensory contact comes it will have an effect. The mind will go out with labels of good and bad, liking and disliking. So make sure you maintain the basic awareness that's aware right at itself. And don't let there be any labeling. No matter what sort of sensory contact comes, you have to make sure that this awareness comes first.

If you train yourself correctly in this way, everything will stop. You won't go straying out through your senses of sight, hearing, and so forth. The mind will stop and look, stop and be aware right at awareness, so as to know the truth that all things arise and disband. There's no real truth to anything. Only our stupidity is what latches onto things, giving them meanings and then suffering for it—suffering because of its ignorance, suffering because of its unacquaintance with the five aggregates—form, feelings, perceptions, thought-fabrications, and consciousness—all of which are inconstant, stressful, and not-self.

Use mindfulness to gather your awareness together, and the mind will stop getting unsettled, stop running after things. It will be able to stop and be still. Then make it know in this way, see in this way *constantly*—at every moment, with every activity. Work at watching and knowing the mind in and of itself: That will cut away all sorts of issues. You won't have to concern yourself with them.

If the body is in pain, simply keep watching it. Simply keep watching feelings in the body, because the mind that's aware of itself can keep watching anything within or without. Or it can simply be aware of itself to the point where it lets go of things outside, lets go of sensory contact, and keeps constant watch on the mind in and of itself. That's when you'll know what the mind is like when it's at peace: It doesn't give meanings to anything. It's the emptiness of the mind, unattached, uninvolved, unconcerned with anything at all.

These words—"unattached," "uninvolved," "unconcerned"—are ones you have to consider carefully, because what they refer to is subtle and deep. "Uninvolved" means uninvolved with sensory contact, undisturbed by the body or feelings. "Unconcerned" means not worried about the past, future, or present. You have to contemplate these things until you know them skillfully. Even though they're subtle, you have to contemplate them until you know them thoroughly. And don't go concerning yourself with external things, because they'll keep you unsettled, keep you running, keep you distracted with labels and thoughts of good and bad and all that sort of thing. You have to put a stop to these things. If you don't, your practice won't accomplish anything, because these things keep deceiving you. When something succeeds in distracting you, it will fool you into seeing it as right, wrong, good, bad, and so forth.

Eventually you have to come down to the awareness that everything simply arises, persists, and then disbands. *Make sure you stay focused on the disbanding.* If you watch just the arising, you may get carried off on a tangent, but if you focus on the disbanding you'll see emptiness: Everything is disbanding every instant. No matter what you look at, no matter what you see, it's there for just an instant and then disbands. Then it arises again. Then it disbands. There's simply arising, knowing, disbanding.

So let's watch what happens of its own accord—because the arising and disbanding that occurs by way of the senses is something that happens on its own. You can't prevent it. You can't force it. If you look and know it without attachment, the mind will be unaffected by the harm that comes from joy or sorrow. It will stay in relative normalcy and neutrality. But if you're forgetful and start latching on, labeling things in pairs—good and bad, happy and sad, pleasing and displeasing—the mind will become unsettled: no longer empty, no longer still. When this happens, you have to probe and find out why.

All the worthless issues that arise in the mind have to be cut away. Then you'll find that you have less and less to say, less and less to talk about, less and less to think about. These things grow less and less on their own. They stop on their own. But if you get involved in a lot of issues, the mind won't be able to stay still. So we have to keep watching things, *things that are completely worthless and without substance,* to see that they're not-self. Keep watching them repeatedly, because your awareness, coupled with the mindfulness and discernment that will know the truth, has to see that "This isn't my self. There's no substance or worth to it at all. It simply arises and disbands right here. It's here for just an instant and then it disbands."

All we have to do is stop and look, stop and know clearly, and we'll be able to do away with many, many kinds of suffering and stress. The normal stress of the aggregates will still occur—we can't prevent it—but we'll know that it's the stress of nature and won't latch onto it as ours.

So we keep watch on things that happen on their own. If we know how to watch, we keep watching things that happen on their own. Don't latch onto things as being "you" or "yours." Keep this awareness firmly centered in itself as much as you can, and there won't be much else you'll have to remember or think about.

When you keep looking, keep knowing like this at all times, you'll come to see that there are no big issues going on. There's just the issue of arising, persisting, and disbanding. You don't have to label anything as good or bad. If you simply look in this way, it's no great weight on the heart. But if you go dragging in issues of good and bad, self and all that, then suffering starts in a big way. The defilements start in a big way and weigh on the heart, making it troubled and upset. So you have to stop and look, stop and investigate really deep down inside. It's like water covered with duckweed. When we push aside the duckweed, we see that the water beneath is crystal clear.

As you look into the mind, you have to push it aside, to stop it: stop thinking, stop labeling things as good or bad, stop everything. You can't go branding everything. Simply keep looking, keep knowing. When the mind is quiet, you'll see that there's nothing there. Everything is all still. Everything has stopped inside. But as soon as there's labeling—even in the stillness—it will set things in motion. And as soon as things are in motion, if you don't know how to let go right away, issues will arise, waves will arise. Once there are issues and waves, they strike the mind, which will go on splashing all out of control. This splashing of the mind includes craving and defilement as well, because *avijjā*—ignorance—lies at its root.

Our major obstacle is this aggregate of perceptions, or labels. If we aren't aware of the arising and disbanding of perceptions, these labels will take hold. Perceptions are the chief instigators that label things, so we have to be aware of their arising and disbanding. Once we're aware in this way, perceptions will no longer cause suffering. In other words, they won't give rise to any further thought-fabrications. The mind will be aware and extinguish them.

So we have to stop things at the level of perception. If we don't, thought-fabrications will fashion them into issues and then cause consciousness to wobble and waver in all sorts of ways. But these are things we can stop and look at, things we can know with every mental moment.

If we aren't yet really acquainted with the arising and disbanding in the mind, we won't be able to let go. We can talk about letting go, but we can't do it because we don't yet know. As soon as anything arises we grab hold of it—even when actually it's already disbanded, but since we don't really see, we don't know....

So I ask that you understand this basic principle. Don't go grasping after this thing or that, or else you'll get yourself all unsettled. The basic theme is within: Keep on looking within, keep on knowing within until you penetrate everything. The mind will then be free from turmoil. Empty. Quiet. Aware. So keep continuous watch on the mind, and you'll come to the point where you simply run out of things to say. Everything will stop on its own, grow still on its own, because the underlying condition—*which has stopped and is still*—is already there. We simply aren't aware of it yet.

THE PURE PRESENT

We have to recognize what if feels like when the mind makes contact with something but isn't aware of itself. Then we'll see how it latches onto things: physical form, feeling, perceptions, thought-fabrications, and consciousness. We ourselves have to probe and look. We can't use the teachings we've memorized to catch sight of these things. That won't get us anywhere at all. We may remember that "the body is inconstant," but even though we can say it, we can't see it.

We have to see exactly *how* the body is inconstant, to see *how* it changes. And we have to focus on feelings—pleasant, painful, and neutral—to see how they change. The same holds true with perceptions, thought-fabrications, and so forth. We have to focus on them, investigate them, contemplate them to see their characteristics *as they actually are.* If you can see these things even for a moment, it'll do you a world of good. You'll be able to catch yourself. What you thought you knew, you didn't really know at all.... This is why the knowledge we gain in the practice has to keep changing through many, many levels. It doesn't stay on just one level.

You may be able to know the arising and disbanding of things in the present, but if your contemplation isn't continuous, it won't be very clear. You have to know how to contemplate the bare sensation of arising and disbanding, simply arising and disbanding, without any labels of "good" or "bad." Just keep with the pure sensation of arising and disbanding. When you do this, other things will intrude—but no matter how they intrude it's still a matter of arising and disbanding, so you can keep your stance with arising and disbanding in this way.

If you start labeling things, it gets confusing. All you need to do is keep looking at the right spot: the bare sensation of arising and disbanding. Simply make sure that you really keep watching it. Whether there's awareness of sights, sounds, smells, tastes, or tactile sensations, just stay with the sensation of arising and disbanding. Don't go labeling the sight, sound, smell, taste, or tactile sensation. If you can keep watch in this way, you're with the pure present— and there won't be any issues.

When you keep watch in this way, you're keeping watch on inconstancy, on change, as it actually occurs—because even the arising and disbanding changes. It's not the same thing arising and disbanding all the time. First this sort of sensation arises and disbands, then that sort arises and disbands. If you keep watch on bare arising and disbanding like this, you're sure to arrive at insight. But if you keep watch with labels—"That's the sound of a cow," "That's the bark of a dog"—you won't be watching the bare sensation of sound, the bare sensation of arising and disbanding. As soon as there's labeling, thought-fabrications come along with it. Your senses of touch, sight, hearing, and so forth will continue their bare arising and disbanding, but you won't know it. Instead, you'll label everything—sights, sounds, etc.—and then there will be attachments, feelings of pleasure and displeasure, and you won't know the truth.

The truth keeps going along on its own. Sensations keep arising and then disbanding. If we focus right here—at the consciousness of the bare sensation of sights, sounds, smells, tastes, and tactile sensations—we'll be able to gain insight quickly.

If we know how to observe things this way, it'll be easy to see when the mind is provoked by passion or greed, and even easier when it's provoked by anger. As for delusion, that's more subtle...something you have to take a great interest in and investigate carefully. You'll come to see all sorts of hidden things—how the mind is covered with many, many layers of film. It's really fascinating. But then, that's what insight meditation is for—to open your eyes so that you can see, so that you can destroy your delusion and ignorance.

THE DECEITS OF KNOWING

You have to find a way to contemplate and probe, so you can catch sight of how, when awareness flickers, it streams out to know things. Be careful to catch sight of it both when its knowing is right and when it's wrong. Don't mix things up, taking wrong knowledge for right, or right knowledge for wrong. This question of right and wrong knowing is extremely important for the practice, for these things can play tricks on you.

When you gain some new insight, don't go getting excited. You can't let yourself get excited by an insight, because it doesn't take long for your insight to change—to change right before your very eyes. It's not going to change at some other time or place. It's changing right now. You have to know how to observe, how to acquaint yourself with the deceits of knowledge. *Even when it's correct knowledge, you can't latch onto it.*

Although you may have standards for judging what sort of knowledge is correct in your practice, don't go latching onto correct knowledge—because correct knowledge is inconstant. It changes. It can turn into false knowledge, or into knowledge that is even more correct. You have to contemplate things very carefully—very, very carefully. Then you won't fall for your own knowledge, thinking, "I've gained right insight; I know better than other people." You won't start assuming yourself to be special. The moment you assume anything about yourself, your knowledge immediately turns wrong. Even if you don't let things show outwardly, the mere mental event in which the mind labels itself is a form of wrong knowing that obscures the mind insidiously.

This is why meditators who tend not to contemplate things, who don't catch sight of the deceit in every form of knowledge—right and wrong, good and bad—tend to get bogged down. The knowledge that deceives them into thinking, "What I know is right," gives rise to strong pride and conceit without their even realizing it.

The defilements are always getting into the act without our realizing it. They're insidious, and in their insidious way they keep getting into the act, for the defilements and mental fermentations are there in our character. Our practice is basically a probing deep inside, from the outer levels of the mind to the inner ones. This is an approach that requires a great deal of subtlety and precision. *The mind must use its own mindfulness and discernment to dig everything out of itself, leaving just the mind in and of itself, the body in and of itself, and then keep watch on them.*

The basic challenge in the practice is this one point and nothing else: *how to look inward so that you see clear through.* If the mind hasn't been trained to look inward, it tends to look outward, simply waiting to receive its objects from outside—and all it gets is the confusion of its sensations going in and out, in and out. And even though this confusion is one aspect of change and inconstancy, we don't see it that way. Instead, we see it as issues, good and bad, pertaining to the self. When this is the case, we're back right where we started, not knowing what's what. This is why the mind's sensations, when it isn't acquainted with itself, are so secretive and hard to perceive. If you try to learn about them by reading books, you end up piling more defilements onto the mind, making it even more thickly covered than before.

So when you turn to look inward, you shouldn't use concepts and labels to do your looking for you. If you use concepts and labels to do your looking, there will be nothing but concepts arising, changing, and disbanding. Everything will get all concocted into thoughts—and then how will you be able to watch in utter silence? The more you take what you've learned from books to look inside yourself, the less you'll see.

So when you come to practice, you have to put aside all the labels and concepts you've learned. You have to be an innocent beginner once more. Only then will you be able to penetrate to the truths within you. If you drag in the paraphernalia of concepts and standards you've learned, you can search until your dying day without meeting with any real truths at all. This is why you have to hold to only one theme in your practice. If the mind concerns itself with lots of themes, it'll just wander around to this and that—going out of bounds without realizing it and not really knowing itself. This is why people with a lot of learning like to teach others, to show off their level of understanding. And this is precisely how the desire to stand out keeps the mind obscured.

Of all the various kinds of deception, *there's none as bad as deceiving yourself.* When you haven't yet really seen the truth, what business do you have making assumptions about yourself, that you've attained this or that sort of knowledge, or that you know enough to teach others correctly? The Buddha is quite critical of teachers of this sort. He calls them "people who live in vain." Even if you can teach large numbers of people to become arahants, so long as you yourself haven't tasted the flavor of the Dhamma, the Buddha says that you're a person who lives in vain. So you have to keep examining yourself. If you haven't trained yourself in what you're teaching to others, how will you extinguish your own suffering?

Think about this for a moment. Extinguishing suffering, gaining release from suffering: Aren't these subtle matters? Aren't they completely personal within us? If you question yourself in this way, you'll be on the right track. But even then you have to be careful. If you start taking sides with yourself, the mind will cover itself up with wrong insights and wrong opinions. If you don't observe really carefully, you can get carried off on a tangent—because the awareness with which the mind reads itself and actually sees through itself is really extraordinary, really worth developing—and it really eliminates suffering and defilement. This is the real, honest truth, not a lot of propaganda or lies. It's something you really have to practice, and then you really have to see clearly in this way. When this is the case, how can you *not* want to practice?

If you examine yourself, you'll know what's real. But you have to examine yourself correctly. If you start latching onto any sense of self, thinking that you're better than other people, then you've failed the examination. No matter how correct your knowledge, you have to stay humble and respectful above all else. You can't let there be any pride or conceit, or it will destroy everything.

This is why the awareness that eliminates the sense of self depends more than anything else on your powers of observation—to check if there's still anything in your knowledge or opinions that comes from the force of pride in any sense of self.... You have to use the full power of your mindfulness and discernment to cut these things away. It's nothing you can play around at. If you gain a few insights or let go of things a bit, don't go thinking you're someone special. The defilements don't hold a truce with anyone. They keep coming right out as they like. So you have to be circumspect and examine things on all sides. Only then will you be able to benefit in ways that make your defilements and sufferings lighter and lighter.

When we probe in to find the instigator—the mind, or this property of consciousness—that's when we're on the right track, and our probing will keep getting results, will keep weakening the germs of craving and wiping them out. In whatever way craving streams out into "being" or "having" in any way at all, we'll be able to catch sight of it. But catching hold and examining this craving for being or having requires a lot of subtlety. If you aren't really mindful and discerning, you won't be able to catch sight of these things at all, because the mind is continually wanting to be and to have. The germs of defilement lie hidden deep in the seed of the mind, in this property of consciousness. Simply to be aware of them skillfully is no mean feat—so we shouldn't even think of trying to wipe them out with our mere opinions. We have to keep contemplating, probing, until things come together just right, in a single moment, and then it's like reaching the basic level of knowing that exists on its own, with no willing or intention at all.

This requires careful observation: the difference between willed and unwilled knowing. Sometimes there's the intention to look within and be aware, but there come times when there's no intention to look within, and yet knowledge arises on its own. If you don't yet know, look at the intention to look inward: What is it like? What is it looking for? What does it see? This is a basic approach you have to hold to. This is a level you have to work at, and one in which you have to make use of intention—the intention to look inward in this way. But once you reach the basic level of knowing, then as soon as you happen to focus and look within, the knowledge will occur on its own.

SABBE DHAMMĀ ANATTĀ

One night I was sitting in meditation outside in the open air—my back straight as an arrow—firmly determined to make the mind quiet, but even after a long time it wouldn't settle down. So I thought, "I've been working at this for many days now, and yet my mind won't settle down at all. It's time to stop being so determined and to simply be aware of the mind." I started to take my hands and feet out of the meditation posture, but at the moment I had unfolded one leg but had yet to unfold the other, I could see that my mind was like a pendulum swinging more and more slowly, more and more slowly—until it stopped.

Then there arose an awareness that was sustained by itself. Slowly I put my legs and hands back into position. At the same time, the mind was in a state of awareness absolutely and solidly still, seeing clearly into the elementary phenomena of existence as they arose and disbanded, changing in line with their nature—and also seeing a separate condition inside, with no arising, disbanding, or changing, a condition beyond birth and death: something very difficult to put clearly into words, because it was a realization of the elementary phenomena of nature, completely internal and individual.

After a while I slowly got up and lay down to rest. This state of mind remained there as a stillness that sustained itself deep down inside. Eventually the mind came out of this state and gradually returned to normal.

From this I was able to observe how practice consisting of nothing but fierce desire simply upsets the mind and keeps it from being still. But when one's awareness of the mind is just right, an inner awareness will arise naturally of its own accord. Because of this clear inner awareness, I was able to continue knowing the facts of what's true and false, right and wrong from that point on, and it enabled me to know that the moment when the mind let go of everything was a clear awareness of the elementary phenomena of nature, because it was an awareness that knew within and saw within of its own accord—not something you can know or see by wanting.

For this reason the Buddha's teaching *"sabbe dhammā anattā—* all phenomena are not-self"—tells us not to latch onto *any* of the phenomena of nature, whether conditioned or unconditioned. From that point on I was able to understand things and let go of attachments step by step.

GOING OUT COLD

It's important to realize how to focus on events in order to get special benefits from your practice. You have to focus so as to observe and contemplate, not simply to make the mind still. Focus on how things arise, how they disband. Make your focus subtle and deep.

When you're aware of the characteristics of your sensations, then—if it's a physical sensation—contemplate that physical sensation. There will be a feeling of stress. When there's stress or pain, can you be aware of it simply as a feeling, so that it doesn't lead to anything further? If you can be aware of it simply as a feeling, it stops right there without producing any taste in terms of a desire for anything. The mind will disengage right there—right there at the feeling. But if you don't focus on it like this, craving will arise on top of the feeling—craving to attain ease and be rid of the stress and pain. If you don't focus on the feeling in the proper way right from the start, craving will arise before you're aware of it, and if you then try to let go of it, it'll be very tiring.

The way preoccupations take shape, the way sensations arise in the mind at every moment, the way these things change and disband—all this you have to focus on and see clearly. This is why we make the mind disengaged. We don't disengage it so that it doesn't know or amount to anything. That's not the kind of disengagement we want. The more the mind is truly disengaged, the more it sees clearly into the characteristics of the arising and disbanding within itself. All I ask is that you observe things carefully, that you keep an all-around awareness at all times. Work at this as much as you can. If you can keep this sort of awareness going, you'll find that the mind or consciousness supervised by mindfulness and discernment is very different from—the very opposite of—unsupervised consciousness. It will be just the opposite sort of thing continually.

If you keep the mind well supervised so that it's sensitive in the proper way, it will yield enormous benefits. If you don't make it properly sensitive and aware, what can you expect to gain?

When we say that we gain from the practice, we're talking about gaining disengagement. Freedom. Emptiness. Before we started to practice, the mind was embroiled. Defilement and craving attacked and robbed it, leaving it completely entangled. Now it's disengaged, freed from the defilements that used to gang up and burn it. Its desires for this or that, its concoction of this or that thought, all have fallen away. So now it's empty and disengaged. It can be empty in this way right before your very eyes. Try to see it right now, before your eyes, right now as I'm speaking and you're listening. Keep probing on in until you see it

If you can be constantly aware in this way, you're following in the footsteps of the Buddha, taking within you the quality called *"buddho,"* which means one who knows, who is awake, who has blossomed in the Dhamma. Even if you haven't fully blossomed— if you've blossomed only to the extent of disengaging from the blatant levels of craving and defilement—you still benefit a great deal, for when the mind really knows the defilements and can let them go, it feels cool and refreshed. This coolness is the exact opposite of the defilements, which, as soon as they arise, make us burn and smolder inside. If we don't have mindfulness and discernment to help us, the defilements will burn us. But as soon as mindfulness and discernment know, the fires go out—and they go out cold.

Observe how the defilements arise and take shape—they also disband in quick succession. But when they go out, when they disband on their own in this way, they go out hot. If we have mindfulness and discernment watching over them, they go out cold. If you look, you'll see what true knowledge is, what mindfulness and discernment are. When true knowledge goes out, it goes out cold. As for the defilements, even when they arise and disband in line with their nature, they go out hot—hot because we latch onto them, hot because of attachment. But when they go out cold, look—it's because there's no attachment. They've been let go, put out.

This is really worth looking into: something very special in the mind—special in that when it really knows the truth, it isn't attached. It's unentangled, empty, and free. That's how it's special. It can grow empty of greed, anger, and delusion, step after step. It can be empty of desire, empty of mental processes. The important thing is that you really see for yourself that the true nature of the mind is that it can be empty.... This is why I've said that *nibbāna* doesn't lie anywhere else. It lies right here, right where things go out and are cool, go out and are cool. It's staring us right in the face.

READING THE HEART

The Buddha taught that we are to know with our own hearts and minds. Even though many, many words and phrases have been coined to explain the Dhamma, we need focus only on the things we can know and see, extinguish and let go of, right in each moment of the immediate present. That's much better than taking on a load of other things. Once we can read and comprehend our inner awareness, we'll understand deep within that the Buddha awakened to the truth right here in the heart. His truth is truly the language of the heart.

When they translate the Dhamma in all sorts of ways, it becomes something ordinary. But if you keep close and careful watch right at the heart and mind, you'll be able to see clearly, to let go, to put down your burdens. If you don't know right here, your knowledge will send out all sorts of branches, turning into thought-fabrications with all sorts of meanings in line with conventional labels—and all of them way off the mark.

If you know right at your inner awareness and make it your constant stance, there's nothing at all: no need to take hold of anything, no need to label anything, no need to give anything names. Right where craving arises, right where it disbands, that's where you'll know what *nibbāna* is like. "*Nibbāna* is simply this disbanding of craving." That's what the Buddha stressed over and over again.

BREATH MEDITATION
CONDENSED

Many people are ashamed to talk about their own defilements but feel no shame at talking about the defilements of others. Those who are willing to report their own diseases—their own defilements—in a straightforward manner are few and far between. As a result, the disease of defilement is hushed up and kept secret, so that we don't realize how serious and widespread it is. We all suffer from it, and yet no one is open about it. No one is really interested in diagnosing his or her own defilements.

We have to find a skillful approach if we hope to wipe out this disease, and we have to be open about it, admitting our defilements from the grossest to the most subtle, dissecting them down to their minutest details. Only then will our practice benefit us. If we look at ourselves superficially, we may feel that we're fine just as we are and that we already know all we need to know. Then when the defilements let loose with full force as anger or delusion, we pretend that nothing is wrong—and this way the defilements become a hidden disease, hard to catch hold of, hard to diagnose.

We have to be strong in fighting off defilements, cravings, and illusions of all sorts. We have to test our strength against them and bring them under our power. If we can bring them under our power, we can ride on their backs. If we can't, they'll ride on *our* backs, making us do their work, pulling us around by the nose, making us want this or that, wearing us out in all sorts of ways.

So are we still beasts of burden? Are defilements and craving riding on our backs? Have they put a ring through our noses? When you get to the point when you've had enough, you have to stop—stop and watch the defilements to see how they come into being, what they want, what they eat, what they find delicious. Make it your sport to watch the defilements and starve them, like someone giving up an addiction. See if it gets the defilements upset. Do they hunger to the point where they're salivating? Then don't let them eat. No matter what, don't let them eat what they're addicted to. After all, there are plenty of other things to eat. You have to be hard on them—hard on your "self"—like this. "Hungry? Well go ahead and be hungry! You're going to die? Fine! Go ahead and die!" If you can take this attitude, you'll be able to win out over all sorts of addictions, all sorts of defilements—because you're not pandering to desire, you're not nourishing the desire that lives only for the sake of finding flavor in physical things. It's time you stopped, time you gave up feeding your defilements. If they're going to waste away and die, let them die. After all, why should you keep them fat and well fed?

No matter what, you have to keep putting the heat on your cravings and defilements until they wither and waste away. Don't let them raise their heads. Keep them under your thumb. This is the sort of straightforward practice you have to follow. If you have enough endurance to fight them persistently until they're all

44

burned away, no other victory will ever match your conquest over the cravings and defilements in your own heart.

This is why the Buddha taught us to put the heat on the defilements in all our activities—sitting, standing, walking, and lying down. If we don't do this, *they'll* burn *us* in all our activities.

If you consider things carefully, you'll see that the Buddha's teachings are exactly right in telling us how to examine our defilements and extinguish them. All the steps are there, so we needn't go study anywhere else. Every point in his doctrine and discipline shows us the way. How we should go about examining and curing this disease becomes mysterious only if you study the Buddha's teachings without making reference to doing away with your own defilements. People don't like to talk about their own defilements, so they end up completely ignorant. They grow old and die without knowing a thing about their own defilements at all.

When in our practice we begin to comprehend how the defilements burn our own hearts, that's when we gradually come to know ourselves. To understand suffering and defilement and learn how to extinguish defilement gives us space to breathe.

When we learn how to put out the fires of defilement, how to destroy them, it means we have the necessary tools. We can be confident in ourselves—no doubts, no straying off into other paths of practice. We know that practicing in this way, contemplating inconstancy, stress, and not-selfness at all times, really gets rid of our defilements.

The same holds true with virtue, concentration, and discernment. They're our tools—and we need a full set. We need the discernment that comes with Right View and the virtue that comes with self-discipline. Virtue is very important. Virtue and discernment are like our right and left hands. If one of our hands is dirty, it can't wash itself. You need to use both hands to keep your hands washed and clean. Thus wherever there's virtue, you have to have discernment. Wherever there's discernment, you have to have virtue. Discernment is what enables you to know; virtue is what enables you to let go, to relinquish, to destroy your addictions. Virtue isn't just a matter of the five or eight precepts, you know. It deals with the finest details. Whatever your discernment sees as a cause of suffering, you have to stop, you have to let go.

Virtue gets very subtle and precise. Letting go, giving up, renouncing, abstaining, cutting away, and destroying: these are all the work of virtue. This is why virtue and discernment go together, just like our right and left hands. They help each other wash away defilement, so your mind can become centered, bright, and clear. The benefits of virtue and discernment become apparent right there in the mind. If we don't have these tools, it's as if we had no hands or feet. We won't be able to go anywhere. We have to use our tools—virtue and discernment—to destroy defilement. That's when our minds will benefit.

This is why the Buddha taught us to keep training in virtue, concentration, and discernment. We have to keep fit through this kind of training. If we don't keep training, our tools for extinguishing suffering and defilement won't be sharp, won't be of much use. They won't be a match for the defilements. The defilements have monstrous powers for burning the mind in the twinkling of an eye. When, say, the mind is quiet and neutral, the slightest sensory contact can set things burning in an instant by making us pleased or displeased. Why?

Sensory contact is our measuring stick for seeing how firm or weak our mindfulness is. Most of the time it stirs things up. As soon as there's contact by way of the ear or eye, the defilements are very quick. How then can we keep things under control? How do we gain control over our eyes? How do we gain control over our ears, nose, tongue, body, and mind? How can we get mindfulness and discernment in charge? This is a matter of practice, pure and simple. It's up to us. We need to test ourselves, to see why defilements flare up so quickly when sensory contact takes place.

Say, for instance, we hear someone criticizing someone else. We can listen and not get upset. But suppose it occurs to us, "Hey, she's actually criticizing *me.*" As soon as we conjure up this "me," we're immediately angry and displeased. If we concoct a lot of this "me," we can get very angry. This alone tells us that as soon as our "self" gets involved, we suffer. This is how it happens. If no sense of self comes out to get involved, we can remain calm and indifferent. When other people are being criticized we can stay indifferent, but as soon as we conclude that we're being criticized, the self appears and immediately gets involved—and we immediately burn with defilement. Why?

You have to pay close attention to this. As soon as the self arises, suffering arises in the very same instant. The same holds true even if you're just thinking. The self you think up spreads out into all sorts of issues. The mind gets scattered all over the place with defilement, craving, and attachments. It has very little mindfulness and discernment watching over it, so it gets dragged every which way by defilement and craving.

And yet we don't realize it. We think we're just fine. Is there anyone among us who realizes that this is what's happening? We're too weighed down, weighed down with our own delusions. No matter how much the mind is smothered in the defilement of delusion, we don't realize it, for it keeps us deaf and blind.

There are no physical tools you can use to detect or cure this disease of defilement, because it arises only at sensory contact. There's no substance to it. It's like a match in a matchbox. As long as the match doesn't come into contact with the friction strip on the side of the box, it won't give rise to fire. But as soon as we strike it against the side of the box, it bursts into flame. If it goes out right then, all that gets burned is the match head. If it doesn't stop at the match head, it'll burn the matchstick. If it doesn't stop with the matchstick, and meets up with anything flammable, it can grow into an enormous fire.

When defilement arises in the mind, it starts from the slightest contact. If we can be quick to put it out right there, it's like striking a match that flares up—*whish!*—for an instant and then dies down right in the match head. The defilement disbands right there. But if we don't put it out the instant it arises and instead let it start concocting issues, it's like pouring fuel onto a fire.

We have to observe the diseases of defilement in our own minds to see what their symptoms are, why they are so quick to flare up. They can't stand to be disturbed. The minute you disturb them, they ignite. When this is the case, what can we do to prepare ourselves? How can we stock up on mindfulness before sensory contact strikes?

The way to stock up is to practice meditation, as we do when we keep the breath in mind. This builds up our mindfulness in advance so that we can keep ahead of defilement. We can keep it from arising as long as we have our theme of meditation as an inner shelter for the mind.

The mind's outer shelter is the body, which is composed of physical elements, but its inner shelter is the theme of meditation we use to train mindfulness to be focused and aware. Whatever theme we use, that's the inner shelter for the mind that keeps it from wandering around, concocting thoughts and imaginings. This is why we need a theme of meditation. Don't let the mind chase after its preoccupations the way ordinary people who don't meditate do. Once we have a meditation theme to catch this monkey of a mind so that it becomes less and less willful day by day, it will calm down, gradually calm down until it can stand firm for longer or shorter periods, depending on how much we train and observe ourselves.

Now for how we *do* breath meditation: The texts say to breathe in long and out long—heavy or light—and then to breathe in short and out short, again heavy or light. Those are the first steps of the training. After that we don't have to focus on the length of the in-breath or out-breath. Instead, we simply gather our awareness at any one point of the breath and keep this up until the mind settles down and is still. When the mind is still, you then focus on the stillness of the mind at the same time you're aware of the breath.

At this point you don't focus directly on the breath. You focus on the mind that is still and at normalcy. You focus continuously on the normalcy of the mind at the same time that you're aware of the breath coming in and out, without actually focusing on the breath. You simply stay with the mind, but you watch it with each in-and-out breath. Usually when you are doing physical work and your mind is at normalcy, you can know what you're doing, so why can't you be aware of the breath? After all, it's part of the body.

Some of you are new at this, which is why you don't know how you can focus on the mind at normalcy with each in-and-out breath without focusing directly on the breath itself. What we're doing here is practicing how to be aware of the body and mind, pure and simple, in and of themselves.

Start out by focusing on the breath for about five, ten, or twenty minutes. Breathe in long and out long, or in short and out short. At the same time notice the stages of how the mind feels, how it begins to settle down when you have mindfulness watching over the breath. You've got to make a point of observing this, because usually when you breathe you do so out of habit, and your attention is far away. You don't focus on the breath; you're not really aware of it. This leads you to think that it's hard to stay focused here, but actually it's quite easy. After all, the breath comes in and out on its own, by its very nature. There's nothing at all difficult about breathing. It's not like other themes of meditation. For instance, if you're going to practice recollection of the Buddha, or *buddho,* you have to keep on repeating *buddho, buddho, buddho.*

Actually, if you want, you can repeat *buddho* in the mind with each in-and-out breath, but only in the very beginning stages. You repeat *buddho* to keep the mind from concocting thoughts about other things. Simply by keeping up this repetition you can weaken the mind's tendency to stray, for the mind can take on only one object at a time. This is something you have to observe. The repetition is to prevent the mind from thinking up thoughts and clambering after them.

After you've kept up the repetition—you don't have to count the number of times—the mind will settle down to be aware of the breath with each in-and-out breath. It will begin to be still, neutral, at normalcy.

This is when you focus on the mind instead of the breath. Let go of the breath and focus on the mind—but still be aware of the breath on the side. You don't have to make note of how long or short the breath is. Make note of the mind that stays at normalcy with each in-and-out breath. Remember this carefully so that you can put it into practice.

The posture: For focusing on the breath, sitting is a better posture than standing, walking, or lying down, because the sensations that come with the other postures often overcome the sensations of the breath. Walking jolts the body around too much, standing for a long time can make you tired, and if the mind gets too settled when you're lying down, you tend to fall asleep. With sitting it's possible to stay in one position and keep the mind firmly settled for a long time. You can observe the subtleties of the breath and the mind naturally and automatically.

Here I'd like to condense the steps of breath meditation to show how all four of the tetrads mentioned in the texts can be practiced at once.* In other words, is it possible to focus on body, feelings, the mind, and dhammas all in one sitting? This is an important question for all of us. You could, if you wanted to, precisely follow all the steps in the texts so as to develop strong powers of mental absorption (jhāna), but it takes a lot of time. It's not appropriate for those of us who are old and have only a little time left.

What we need is a way of gathering our awareness at the breath long enough to make the mind firm, and then go straight to examining how all fabrications are inconstant, stressful, and not-self, so that we can see the truth of all fabrications with each in-and-out breath. If you can keep at this continually, without break, your mindfulness will become firm and snug enough to give rise to the discernment that will enable you to gain clear knowledge and vision.

* The Discourse on Mindfulness of Breathing sets out sixteen steps for practicing breath meditation and then divides the steps into four tetrads, each tetrad dealing with one of the themes mentioned in the Discourse on the Establishing of Mindfulness: body, feelings, mind, and dhammas.

So what follows is a guide to the steps in practicing a condensed form of breath meditation. Try them until they give rise to knowledge within you, knowledge of your very own.

The first thing to remember when you're going to meditate on the breath is to sit straight and keep your mindfulness firm. Breathe in. Breathe out. Make the breath feel open and at ease. Don't tense your hands, your feet, or any of your joints. Keep your body in a posture that feels appropriate to your breathing. At the beginning, breathe in long and out long, fairly heavily, and gradually the breath will shorten—sometimes it will be heavy and sometimes light. Then breathe in short and out short for about ten or fifteen minutes and then allow the breath to change.

After a while, when you stay focused mindfully on it, the breath will gradually change of its own accord. Watch it change for as many minutes as you like, then be aware of the whole breath, all of its subtle sensations. This is the third step, the third step of the first tetrad: *sabba-kāya-paṭisaṁvedī*—focusing on how the breath affects the whole body by watching all the breath sensations in the various parts of the body, and in particular the sensations related to the in-and-out breath.

From there you focus on the sensation of the breath at any one point. When you do this correctly for a fairly long while, the body—the breath—will gradually grow still. The mind will grow calm. In other words, as the breath grows still, so does the awareness of the breath. When the subtleties of the breath grow still, at the same time that your undistracted awareness settles down, the breath grows even stiller. All the sensations in the body gradually grow more and more subtle and still. This is the fourth step, the stilling of bodily fabrication.

As soon as this happens, you begin to be aware of the feelings that arise with the stilling of the body and mind. Whether they're feelings of pleasure or rapture or whatever, they appear clearly enough for you to contemplate them.

The stages through which you have already passed—watching the breath come in and out, long or short—should be enough for you to realize—even though you may not have focused on the idea—that the breath is inconstant. It's continually changing, from in long and out long to in short and out short, from heavy to light, and so forth. This should enable you to read the breath, to understand that there's nothing constant to it at all. It changes on its own from one moment to the next.

Once you've realized the inconstancy of the body—in other words, of the breath—you'll be able to see the subtle sensations of pleasure and pain in the realm of feeling. So now you watch feelings, right there in the same place where you have been focusing on the breath. Even though they are feelings that arise from the stillness of the body or mind, they're nevertheless inconstant even in that stillness. They can change. So these changing sensations in the realm of feeling exhibit inconstancy in and of themselves, just like the breath.

When you see change in the body, change in feelings, and change in the mind, this is called *seeing the Dhamma*—in other words, seeing inconstancy. You have to understand this correctly. Practicing the first tetrad of breath meditation contains all four tetrads of breath meditation. In other words, you see the inconstancy of the body and then contemplate feeling. You see the inconstancy of feeling and then contemplate the mind. The mind, too, is inconstant. This inconstancy of the mind is the Dhamma. To see the Dhamma is to see this inconstancy.

When you see the true nature of all inconstant things, then keep track of that inconstancy at all times, with every in-and-out breath. Keep this up in all your activities to see what happens next.

What happens next is dispassion. Letting go. This is something you have to know for yourself.

This is what condensed breath meditation is like. I call it condensed because it contains all the steps at once. You don't have to do one step at a time. Simply focus at one point, the body, and you'll see the inconstancy of the body. When you see the inconstancy of the body, you'll have to see feeling. Feeling will have to show its inconstancy. The mind's sensitivity to feeling, or its thoughts and imaginings, are also inconstant. All of these things keep on changing. This is how you know inconstancy.

If you can become skilled at looking and knowing in this way, you'll be struck with the inconstancy, stressfulness, and not-selfness of your "self," and you'll meet with the genuine Dhamma. The Dhamma that's constantly changing, like a burning fire—burning with inconstancy, stress, and not-selfness—is the Dhamma of the impermanence of all fabrications. But further within, in the mind or in the property of consciousness, is something special, beyond the reach of any kind of fire. Here there's no suffering or stress of any kind. You could say that this "something special" lies within the mind, but it isn't really in the mind. It's simply that the contact is there at the mind. There's no way you can really describe it. Only the extinguishing of all defilement will lead you to know it for yourself.

This "something special" exists by its very nature, but defilements have it surrounded on all sides. All these counterfeit things—the defilements—keep getting in the way and take possession of everything, so that this special nature remains imprisoned inside. Actually, there's nothing in the dimension of time that can be compared with it. There's nothing by which you can label it, but it's something that you can pierce through to see—by piercing through defilement, craving, and attachment into the state of mind that is pure, bright, and silent. This is the only thing that's important.

But it doesn't have only one level. There are many layers. You go through the outer bark to the inner bark and on to the sapwood before you reach the heartwood. The genuine Dhamma is like the heartwood, but there's a lot to the mind that isn't heartwood. The roots, the branches, and leaves are more than many, but there's only a little heartwood. The parts that aren't heartwood will gradually decay and disintegrate, but the heartwood doesn't decay. That's one kind of comparison we can make. When a tree dies the leaves wither, the branches drop, the bark and sapwood rot, and eventually nothing is left but the true heartwood. That's one comparison we can make with this thing we call deathless, this property that has no birth, no death, no changing. We can also call it *nibbāna* or the Unconditioned. It's all the same thing.

Now then, isn't this something worth trying to see?

GOING AGAINST
THE FLOW

SELF AND SELFISHNESS

You have to examine yourself and take stock of the gains and losses in your practice each step along the way. Then you'll be able to correct, as much as you can, any missteps or lapses in your daily life. If your examination isn't precise, your mind will start backsliding through selfishness. Only when you get down to the details can you keep this disease of selfishness from spreading its germs everywhere.

This is why you have to keep looking inward. If you're caught off guard and a sense of self does arise, you must be sure to wipe it out, especially when it comes in full force. Even when it's subtle, you must still try to catch sight of it, for if you don't wipe out this inner disease completely, your practice won't be in line with the Lord Buddha's teachings.

So you need to make a thorough self-examination, starting from the five and eight precepts. Normally, the precepts can reduce selfishness at a beginning level and boost concentration at an intermediate level. This is something we all understand. Ultimately, though, we have to use mindfulness and discernment to eradicate the "self" that comes from not seeing the truths of inconstancy, stress, and not-self. These are themes we need to contemplate again and again and again.

As we become more and more interested in this, we can begin to eliminate defilement, craving, and clinging, together with our sense of self in its various forms—because our ignorance that things are inconstant and undependable is what gives rise to the desire to hold on to them in the first place.

This disease is hard to treat simply because we're so prone to examining other people instead of ourselves! The act of turning inward, examining ourselves, and catching sight of the "self" hiding insidiously deep within us requires mindfulness and discernment that are subtle and strong. Even then it isn't easy, for we tend to see only the self's deceptions. So we have to examine carefully the many different guises that this sense of self can take. Otherwise, if we don't reflect carefully, our practice will wander off course and end up actually strengthening our sense of self instead of weakening it.

To begin with—so as not to feed this sense of self—we need to be content with what we have. We shouldn't let ourselves feel greed for things, however crude or refined, no matter how much we may feel attracted to them. This is something we each have to see and understand for ourselves—and it isn't easy, as greed can be subtle and insidious. What makes this task even more difficult is that our sense of self is always looking for things to distract us. If we ask what it's hungering for, what it's all worked up about, it just pretends not to hear. It's interested only in wanting more and more, without end.

To be clever in acquiring things is a basic aspect of human nature. The defilements are adept only at getting, but not in giving up or making sacrifices. *If only this could be turned around so that we could become adept at giving away!* It would do so much good, because we would then stop grasping at things and—gradually, with strong contemplation—destroy our attachments. If, by cutting off their food, we stop the defilements from taking their fill, we're following in the footsteps of the arahants. But the other path, the way of deception and fostering "self," puts us in the footsteps of Māra—the defilements personified—and instead of giving away, we're involved only in the endless getting and consuming of things.

So there are these two paths, and you should ask yourself, "Am I really following the path to Awakening or the path of Māra and selfishness? Which path am I more skilled at?" This is a question we have to keep asking ourselves. If we aren't sharp enough, we'll be fooled by the deceptions of the "self," the whispers of Māra that say, "The more I can get, the better." So we have to examine ourselves to see this acute case of selfishness—this adeptness at *getting*—that infects us, each and every one.

As for the storehouse of goods that have been donated for the general use of those who come here to practice, you should be careful never to take anything on your own. Always ask first. If you take this or that so as to be as comfortable as possible, this becomes— even though you may have acted unthinkingly—the same as theft. So don't take any communal property without permission. In fact, you should periodically bring out and share the things donated to you personally. This way you avoid attachment and don't plan just for your own convenience. Otherwise the instinct of self—which loves to appropriate things—will get so adept that you'll have trouble seeing its dangers.

If we make the mistake of accepting the principle "The more I can get, the better," we put ourselves under the power of Māra. Now that we've become disciples of the Lord Buddha, how can we possibly let ourselves do that? If we see any particularly strong greed arising within us, then the only way out is to give up its object. Give it away! Under no circumstances at all should you take it surreptitiously. I tell you plainly: Anyone living in a religious community who behaves like this will go only from bad to worse, because she has no sense of shame or fear of the consequences of evil. Without these two fundamental principles as a foundation, how can we possibly build up the Dhamma within us? Even though we might be expert in citing and reciting the scriptures, if we can't straighten out even such a basic flaw, the mind will know no bounds to its greed. It will get really ugly—or, at least, the disease that infects it will. And what can we do to cleanse it? To associate with extremely selfish people will simply inflame the disease all the more and spread its infection deep into the heart.

This subject of greed is one that people tend to keep hidden and don't like to talk about. It's not a pleasant topic at all, because of its insidious implications. Only by using mindfulness and discernment in examining ourselves will we be able to know the deceits of greed and defilement. How can they be destroyed? Not by being half-hearted, that's for sure. You have to give up as much as possible. If anything provokes selfishness, give it up. You shouldn't agree among yourselves that each can grab as much as she can, but instead you should encourage one another to give as much as you can. If you don't, then the mind will become inflamed because you infect yourself with the dirt and disease of selfishness. And who can possibly come to treat you?

Remember this when you decide to examine this deadly disease in the mind, for no one else will want to discuss it with you. Even though others are all filled with the same germs, they prefer to talk of other things. Giving away material things from time to time is relatively easy, *but to relinquish the "self" is both profound and extremely hard.* Still, it's worth the effort, because this sense of self is the sole source of all suffering. If its roots aren't destroyed, it will continue to sprout and flourish. So we have to turn and look inward to catch it.

The Lord Buddha laid down the Recollection of the Four Requisites, which are—for the monks—robe cloth, alms food, shelter, and medicine. He said that if these things weren't considered merely as material supports, as physical elements free of all notion of self, then they'd be as hot as fire. Now, we ourselves aren't monks and may only be beginners in the practice, but if we're really determined to destroy the defilements and the sense of self, it doesn't hurt to try following the same practice. If we don't, just imagine how defilement, craving, clinging, and our sense of self will grow without bounds.

So you have to choose: to follow your old ways or to make the effort to turn toward putting an end to this sense of self. This is very much your own personal concern. Turning inward to examine yourself goes against the grain, but if you try, even only a little, the benefits will be enormous. When you can actually catch the deceit of self in the act of pulling you still deeper into suffering, and can wipe it out then and there, the rewards are truly beyond price.

If we don't succeed in wiping out this sense of self, then the seed for continued suffering gets planted and grows. And if we don't turn inward to examine it, it'll proliferate. Even though we can cite and recite the scriptures, and even teach others skillfully, the mind is still impure and confused. But when we can see all this clearly, we'll feel disgust for our desires. We'll begin to give things up and make sacrifices—however difficult they may seem—so as not to allow suffering to take hold. In this way, each small renunciation builds its own reward in the mind until there's total victory.

Those of us with a strong tendency to stinginess, which is a defilement pure and simple, are unable to give up anything. We're reluctant to look at ourselves and admit that we have the severe diseases listed in the Sixteen Corruptions *(upakkilesa)* and the various precepts. If we examine ourselves frequently and carefully, such defilements don't dare show their faces; but if we're careless, the defilements grow bold and are capable of the most selfish and despicable acts. We then find it easy to appropriate for our own purposes the property of a community such as we have here. When we turn inward, constantly trying to examine our minds and giving up our worthless attachments, then whatever we do will be Dhamma—and a help to our companions in birth, aging, illness, and death. Once we uproot our selfishness, we can help others with no concern for the hardships involved. *When we're free from the sense of self, we're truly on the noble path.*

The practice of Dhamma requires a basic orderliness in daily life. Without that orderliness, our practice becomes unseemly. Sloppiness in our behavior allows the defilements to arise more easily. Orderliness helps to arouse mindfulness, which enables us to block them. Rules and regulations, if we disregard them, can accomplish nothing; but if we abide by them conscientiously, they're very beneficial. They help provide us with a sense of how to respond correctly to every situation—something we need because we don't yet really understand by ourselves. The Lord Buddha knew all situations from all angles, whereas we're surrounded by darkness and ignorance on all sides. We can't be sure of ourselves with regard to matters within us or without, so we have to depend on the Dhamma as our guide. But whether we're going to follow the Dhamma or wander astray is something we each must decide for ourselves.

If we're not complacent, if we want to get rid of our defilements, suffering, and stress, then we have to set ourselves to the task and stick with it. Whichever way we've turned, we've met nothing but the fire of suffering, so now it's time to stop, turn inward, and devote ourselves to fighting to be free. If we don't have a clear and thorough understanding of our minds, the defilements will thrive and spread their germs, bringing nothing but more and more suffering. So we have to strengthen our mindfulness and discernment, for no other tools can fight the defilements and destroy them.

This calls for a relentless effort to train the mind, with mindfulness and discernment pointing the way. Halfheartedness is simply a waste of time and leaves us as stupid as before. When we realize this, the benefits from our effort will grow until eventually we can destroy the defilements, relinquish our attachments, and gain release from all suffering. But if we don't work in this direction, we'll be swept away by the power of craving and defilement. If we're complacent and careless, the defilements will drag us around by the nose, pulling us here and there, which is why the Lord Buddha recommended relinquishment, sacrifice, and disengagement as tools for removing the virulent diseases in the mind.

These diseases are very insidious. Sometimes they show their true nature a little, but rarely enough to alert us. This is why they eventually take over. And sometimes we even gladly submit to them! So our examination needs to be very careful, very circumspect. Otherwise it's like plugging one hole in a leaking boat only to find another leak someplace else. There are six holes or apertures—the senses of sight, hearing, smell, taste, feeling, and ideation—and if we don't keep watch over them, they're left open for the mind to stream out after objects that can make it suffer even more.

So we have to use mindfulness and discernment to take stock of what's actually going on within ourselves. This should take priority as our most important task throughout the day. *Our life is for working on the elimination of defilement, not for anything else.* Yet defilement and suffering continue to lie in wait and will burn us if we aren't equal to them. We have to turn ourselves around and ask how we can get out of this situation. This is what will lead to great results. While we still have breath, and our bodies are not yet rotting in their coffins, we must look for advice and search for a way to eradicate the causes of these terrible diseases: the germs of defilement and craving. These diseases eat deeply into the mind and can be cured only with the Dhamma. From the various Dhamma medicines the Lord Buddha prescribed, we must each carefully choose the ones appropriate to our situation, and then use them—with genuine circumspection—to destroy our diseases at their root.

As long as our self-inspection isn't up to destroying the defilements, they'll grow stronger and burn like a smoldering fire inside the mind. Self-inspection is the extinguisher we use to snuff out greed. After we use it, we check the mind again: Is it really free or has it flared up once more? If we don't keep at this, we can only end up getting consumed by the flames. No matter how smart we think we are, we let greed take charge and make no attempt to uproot it. We even go out to welcome it with open arms! Our mind thus becomes a slave to desire. It falls into delusion, grasping this and that, and ends up entrapped, without a clue as to how to get out of its predicament.

Stymied by our lack of genuine resolve, and at our wits' end, we fall back to being slaves to the defilements. The more often we submit to them, the stronger they grow. The only real way to over-throw them is to rouse our mindfulness and discernment to with-stand and examine—from every angle—the suffering that the defilements bring, until the mind refuses to remain a slave any longer. There's no use in just making an external show of it, because the greater the fuss, the more stubborn the defilements become. So we can't be halfhearted. We need an *appropriate* response for whatever the situation. Good intentions aren't enough. What's needed is for us to focus and intensify our mindfulness and discernment with great care and circumspection. This is an impor-tant point, so be sure to remember it well.

For the mind to gain genuine understanding, it has to keep investigating your every activity with every breath. It'll then be equal to the task of stopping your preoccupations and your contin-ual tendency to fabricate worthless ideas under the force of delu-sion. When you're not really determined, your practice becomes halfhearted and ends up scattered—a waste of valuable time. So look inside yourself and keep on looking until you see clearly.

Actually, once you're adept, it's more fun to look inside than out. Outside, there's nothing to see but things passing away, pass-ing away. What's so enthralling about that? But the inner eye can penetrate to the clear light within and then to the truth of the Dhamma. Once we see the nature of the passing away of all fabri-cated things, we'll gain new insight into the nature that doesn't pass away: a nature that can't change, but simply is.

As long as our mindfulness and discernment are still inadequate and lack support, the defilements will overpower us. But if we're persistent in strengthening mindfulness and discernment, the defilements will gradually weaken and fade. We then begin notic-ing how the mind that used to be confused and uncertain is now confident and clear. It sees the inconstancy of things more precisely. It can let them go. This insight into inconstancy enables our mindfulness and discernment to penetrate to deeper and deeper insight. But this penetration has to be really focused and continuous, for the slightest lapse in attention will disrupt it. Only when it doesn't waver or wander off target, even for a moment, can it bring the defilements under control. If it's careless, it can never affect them, and they'll regroup stronger than before.

So develop mindfulness and alertness in your every activity, with every breath. Make the effort to keep the mind attentive so that it doesn't drift away after its preoccupations or get fooled by its imaginings. *And beware of the tendency to think "I know" when you really don't.* Until the mind penetrates to true insight, there will always be doubt and uncertainty, but when you truly start to see, doubts fall away and you no longer speculate about things. You truly know.

Right now, though, can you be sure that your insight is true? When the mind really sees, then defilement, suffering, and stress are really eliminated; but if you just think you see, with no real insight into the mind, then defilement and suffering can't possibly be destroyed.

True insight penetrates into the mind, where desires keep arising and the things that obstruct the Dhamma dwell. Only when you can stop these things from forming can you see the nature of a mind that's free from the fire and anguish of desire. This you can see anytime—when you focus properly and with determination. Other things you can see, so why not this? Just take a good look and you're sure to see! But if you're going to penetrate, you have to look in an *appropriate* way. Otherwise you'll see nothing. If you grasp at things—in defiance of the basic principles of true knowledge—and then try to go straight to the truth, everything will get twisted, and an element of pride or something of the sort will worm its way in.

The only safe path is to watch the arising and passing away of things—simply watch and know without grasping. So look! This is the way to freedom from attachment. The Buddha said, "See the world as empty." That's how we have to view our preoccupations as they arise and pass away: as empty. When the mind truly understands the inconstancy of things—the deceits of the world and our preoccupations—it doesn't latch onto them any more. This is the empty mind. The free mind. There are many levels to this emptiness, but even a brief taste of any of them is very beneficial. Just don't go grasping after anything!

This empty mind, this free mind, is called *vimokkha*—true and final liberation. It's described in one of the scriptures we chant, the Soḷasa Pañhā (Sutta Nipāta V): "*Vimokkha* is not affected by change." The levels of the empty mind that change aren't true *vimokkha*, so we have to keep examining each level and press for the result, which is always freedom from attachment, regardless of how many levels we have to work through until the mind finally doesn't change, when it has no label or attachment for anything at all. This is the true way to penetrating insight.

May all of you who practice the Dhamma strive without tiring until you come to see and know this truth for yourselves.

A SENSE OF PRIORITIES

We all suffer from stress and pain, and our most important task in life is to get rid of it. If our minds lack knowledge of the Dhamma, we're left helpless in the face of the defilements causing that stress.

Unless we turn to the Dhamma, we'll be consumed throughout this life and on into the next. Only Dhamma practice—and nothing else—can extinguish defilement and release us from suffering.

Basically, Dhamma practice means constantly looking inward at our own body and mind, for the body and mind are the basis of our existence. The way they change by their very nature is something we have to investigate in an appropriate way, for otherwise we'll follow the unthinking, *ordinary* way, understanding nothing and latching onto things that can only increase our suffering. The cause of suffering is difficult to see and requires our full attention. When we examine the restlessness and anxiety of the mind, we find that it comes from the diseases of greed, aversion, and delusion. To desire things brings nothing but turmoil to the mind, which is like infecting it with a virulent disease.

Normally, we're afraid of physical diseases, but the diseases of defilement that soil the mind don't concern us at all. We're unwilling to realize how serious they are; and sometimes, in our ignorance, we make them even worse. For this reason, actually getting down to the nitty-gritty of eliminating the defilements is difficult and unappealing, especially in the face of the many, many outside distractions that stir up desire. Ordinary—oblivious—people just spin along with their desires, making themselves dizzy and losing their balance all the time. This is obviously suffering and stress, yet if we don't concern ourselves with this affliction, don't struggle to overcome the tendency to follow desire, we have to submit to it. Our ignorance of the fact that the defilements have already overpowered and infected the mind is what makes these diseases so difficult to see.

So we have to turn our attention from outside things and focus it on our own body and mind. Body and mind, form and name—whatever you call them—are all subject to inconstancy and change, but this is hard for ordinary people to realize. It's like what we think of as the growth of a person. From the first days in your mother's womb onward, there's continual change and transformation. Growth simply means change. There's nothing in the world not subject to change.

The deterioration of the body and material things shouldn't be so difficult to notice, but still it escapes our attention. Mental states are also constantly changing, yet instead of seeing this whenever we come into contact with sights or sounds, we only grasp at the object, and this sinks us even deeper into suffering and stress.

If we could penetrate into the experience of sights, sounds, smells, tastes, tactile sensations, and ideas, we'd find a constant change, a constant arising and passing away. How does an old preoccupation pass away? How does a new one arise in its place? How do the defilements force the mind to produce concepts and imaginings that proliferate out of bounds? We pay no attention to these matters and so find ourselves overwhelmed by the stress that results in words and deeds full of intense greed, aversion, and delusion.

The torment caused by the defilements—hotter than the hottest fire—can be relieved only through the practice of Dhamma. But ordinary, run-of-the-mill people, even though they're being roasted alive, behave as if they're immune to the fire and pay it no mind. They even smile and content themselves with grasping at fleeting things as "me" and "mine." They don't realize that whatever they love and grasp at is forever slipping out of reach, forever dissolving away.

We have to look inward as deeply as possible so that we can see the truth and not fall into delusion or attachment. We read in the canon about such diseases as the fetters (saṅyojana) or obsessions (anusaya), but we don't turn to check for them in ourselves. We may translate the words and know their meanings, but we don't see that *sakkāya-diṭṭhi* (personal identity views) are the direct source of all our suffering and torment. Not only do we misconstrue the plain truth, we're perfectly willing to hold on to our wrong views without examining them. This is why the mind is so deeply ignorant.

People in general know about many, many things, sometimes to the point where they can't sit still and always have to be researching new topics. They know what's good, what's right—they know everything! Whatever the subject, they manage to concoct an answer until their ideas run all out of bounds. *They simply know too much.* This kind of knowledge is the knowledge coming from defilement and craving. Its antidote is the knowledge coming from mindfulness and discernment penetrating into the truth of the mind. If we give free rein to our obsession with discursive thinking, the mind will wear itself out, and eventually we'll suffer a nervous breakdown. If we let this happen, we'll end up insane—maybe staying deluded till death and returning to that same delusion upon being reborn. This is because we haven't used the Dhamma to examine and disband that thinking. Drugs or tranquilizers relieve only the external symptoms and don't get to the root cause. To get to the root, we need to use mindfulness and discernment to supervise the mind so that it can free itself from its delusions. This is how the Dhamma effects its complete cure.

The fact that Dhamma practice is able to cure every disease of the mind should merit some thought. Each stage in our understanding of the Dhamma depends on mindfulness and discernment. If we show no interest in Dhamma—no matter how great our knowledge of worldly matters—we fall under the power of the defilements, subject to birth, aging, illness, and death. Once we understand the Dhamma in line with the Buddha, though, our minds will become bright, calm, and pure. This knowledge is far more precious than the skills we acquire for making a living or for finding entertainment.

When we come to examine our minds constantly, we see that when the mind becomes restless, it loses its freedom and refuses to accept the Lord Buddha's instructions: "See security in the renunciation of sensuality." Being burned alive by trying to find gratification in sensual objects—sights, sounds, smells, tastes, and tactile sensations—is certainly not "seeing security in the renunciation of sensuality." But if we correctly see that the penalty of sensuality is suffering and stress, then we no longer content ourselves with it, and the mind is set free. At that moment, when the mind is unattached to sense objects and is free of desire, we can penetrate to more profound levels and know for ourselves whether there really is any happiness in sensuality. The free mind will know in and of itself that happiness lies in not being overwhelmed by suffering or aroused to passion. The mind without passion will immediately incline solely toward freedom. Is this what you want, or are you content with your insatiable desires? Think carefully about this and make your choice.

Inclining the mind toward freedom from its entanglement in sensuality brings a natural state of purity and calm. Compared to this freedom and ease, the thought of being embroiled in sensuality is bound to seem unappealing. If you don't reflect on this, you stay lost in desires and passions without end, imprisoned in craving. You've been trapped so long by this disease so difficult to cure. Isn't it high time you made up your mind to destroy it at its root?

When the mind labels and latches onto an object it desires, you should reflect and see the harm and suffering that arise as a result. Then compare this unease with the ease of the mind freed from desire. You have to keep contemplating these two states—suffering and freedom from suffering—in your own mind, keeping track of them with every in-and-out breath. This principle is set out in the Discourse on the Establishing of Mindfulness, which describes many different ways to examine and reflect. But if you don't actually apply them in your practice, they won't benefit you at all, no matter how many texts you read. You'll just keep groping along in the dark, understanding nothing.

To detect this disease, you need to foster mindfulness and discernment, putting them to use until they become firmly established. If you put them to use only sporadically and halfheartedly, you'll stay stuck in complacency and will never make any progress in the practice. Yet it's just this very progress that leads to a reduction in desire, suffering, and stress. This you'll need to see for yourself: The most direct way to practice is to reflect and examine things constantly. See how you can best apply the practice of reflection to your daily life.

Those of us here who devote our lives to the Dhamma by living the holy life have to be especially scrupulous about this point. Our practice requires that we make earnest use of mindfulness and discernment, sticking with it until true knowledge arises. We start by learning how to investigate so that new understanding will arise in place of our ignorance. As long as the mind is possessed by ignorance and delusion, we can't relax or be complacent. We have to concern ourselves persistently with escaping from whatever brings suffering and stress, and with discerning what brings brightness and clarity to the mind.

If we don't, the mind will tend to be hoodwinked by the sense objects around it, and our practice will end up in just theories and words. The fact of the matter is that our mind doesn't really know what's what. Any scrap of genuine insight that *does* arise, we don't follow up. We sit back, letting ourselves get preoccupied with things outside and neglecting the practice. So we need to watch out for complacency, exercising our mindfulness and discernment so that they can steadily develop. When we can penetrate to the truths of inconstancy, stress, and not-selfness even if just for a moment, we see that this is really the perfect way to disband all suffering and stress. If there's anything we don't yet discern, we have to investigate it earnestly and compare it to what we already know. This leads to disengagement from "self" and "others," from "mine" and "theirs." Even just a momentary insight gives value to our life. Without it, we remain in the continual darkness of ignorance and ceaseless imaginings that keep the mind trapped in a constant turmoil—a wretched state of affairs.

So instead of being concerned only with eating and sleeping and other ordinary activities, we have to steadily develop our meditation. Make sure that the mind stays under the supervision of mindfulness and discernment, always within the bounds of restraint. Don't ever send it out after other matters that are a waste of time.

A first step in the practice is to follow the precepts. We need to do this because otherwise things simply get confused. As we submit to the precepts and discipline, we find that they bring great rewards. We then come to see that the purpose of life is simply to train ourselves to eliminate defilement and suffering before the body is laid out in its coffin. If the mind isn't this concerned about finding a suitably quiet place and practicing, it will tend to go all out of bounds with its thoughts and ideas. So we must each resolve on our course, blocking the mind when it wanders after sense objects and preoccupations, and bringing it back to investigate within so as to steadily develop tranquillity and calm.

The Lord Buddha set down a variety of correct methods, such as mindfulness of breathing, that are just right for developing mental calm. If we don't take one of these methods as a basis for practice, then any results will be unstable and fleeting. But if we use them, our minds can be brought under the control of mindfulness and alertness without blurring into distraction.

How should we each go about this to obtain the results we want? How can we improve our practice in our daily life? These are all questions we should ponder with care. Don't be complacent and forgetful. Everything we do in the practice—including guarding the sense doors—we must stick to tenaciously without wavering or straying away. Otherwise time flies by, our life ebbs away, and we accomplish nothing. If you're inattentive and halfhearted, how can you expect to escape from suffering? What a waste!

So be earnest! If you're really earnest, you'll be able to set yourself aright and steadily wear away your tendency to be distracted. Center your investigation on inconstancy, the stress inherent in that inconstancy, and the not-selfness of it all. Then focus back on the center of your awareness and penetrate so as to clearly understand those themes as they apply to the mind as well as the body. When you succeed in clearly realizing this, you can truly be called wise, awakened, happy in the Dhamma. If your insight is genuine, you'll be free from feelings of "me" and "mine," with no attachment or involvement with anything at all.

Does this sound interesting? I'm not speaking of trivial matters, you know. I'm speaking frankly of serious matters, and you should pay serious attention. Listening absentmindedly serves no purpose at all. You have to make the effort to gain insight within yourself. This brings such great rewards that you should make it your primary concern. Focus on this above all else.

May the Dhamma become the guiding light in your life.

MINDFULNESS LIKE
THE PILINGS OF A DAM

Discussing the practice is more useful than discussing anything else because it gives rise to insight. If we follow the practice step by step, we can *read* ourselves, continually deciphering things within us. As you read yourself through probing and investigating the harm and suffering caused by defilement, craving, and attachment, there will be times when you come to true knowledge, enabling you to grow dispassionate and let go. The mind will then immediately grow still, with none of the mental concoctions that used to have the run of the place through your lack of self-investigation.

The principles of self-investigation are our most important tools. We have to make a concerted effort to master them, especially our use of mindfulness to focus on the mind and bring it to centered concentration. If we don't focus on keeping the mind centered or neutral as its basic stance, it will wander off in pursuit of preoccupations or sensory contacts, giving rise to turmoil and restlessness. But when we practice restraint over the sensory doors by maintaining continuous mindfulness in the heart, it's like driving in the pilings for a dam. If you've ever seen the pilings for a dam, you'll know that they're driven deep, deep into the ground so that they're absolutely firm and immovable. But if you drive them into mud, they're easily swayed by the slightest contact. This should give us an idea of how firm our mindfulness should be in stabilizing the mind, enabling it to withstand sensory contact without liking or disliking its objects.

The firmness of your mindfulness is something you have to maintain continuously in your every activity, with every in-and-out breath, so the mind ceases its scattered pursuit of preoccupations. If you don't manage this, the mind will get stirred up whenever there's sensory contact, like a rudderless ship going wherever the wind and waves take it. This is why you need mindfulness to guard the mind at every moment. If you can make mindfulness constant, in every activity, the mind will be continuously neutral, ready to probe and investigate for insight.

As a first step in driving in the pilings for your dam—in making mindfulness firm—focus on neutrality as your basic stance. There's nothing you have to think about. Simply make the mind solid in its neutrality. If you can do this continuously, that's when you'll have a true standard for your investigation, because the mind will have gathered into concentration. But this concentration is something you have to watch over carefully to make sure it's not just oblivious indifference. Make the mind firmly established and centered so that it doesn't get absentminded or distracted as you sit in meditation. Sit straight, maintain steady mindfulness, and there's nothing else you have to do. Keep the mind firm and neutral, not thinking of anything at all. Make sure this stability stays continuous. When anything pops up, no matter how, keep the mind neutral. For example, if there's a feeling of pleasure or pain, don't focus on the feeling. Simply focus on the stability of the mind—and there will be a sense of neutrality in that stability.

If you're careful not to let the mind get absentminded or distracted, its concentration will become continuous. For example, if you're going to sit for an hour of meditation, focus on centering the mind like this for the first half hour and then make sure it doesn't wander off anywhere until the hour is up. If you change positions, it's simply an outer change in the body, while the mind stays firmly centered and neutral each moment you're standing, sitting, lying down, or whatever.

Mindfulness is the key factor in all of this, keeping the mind from concocting thoughts or labeling things. *Everything has to stop.* Keep this foundation snug and stable with every in-and-out breath. Then relax your focus on the breath while keeping the mind neutral. If your focus is heavy, relax so that it feels just right with the breath. The mind will be able to stay in this state for the entire hour, free from any thoughts that might lead it off the path. Then keep an eye out to see that no matter what you do or say, the mind stays solidly in its normal state of inward knowing.

If the mind is stable within itself, you're protected on all sides. When sensory contacts come, you stay focused on being aware of your mental stability. Even if there are any momentary slips in your mindfulness, you get right back to the stability of the mind. Other than that, there's nothing you have to do. The mind will let go without your having to do anything else. The mind used to engage in liking this and hating that, turning left here and turning right there, but now this won't happen. It will stay neutral, equanimous, just right. If mindfulness lapses, you get right back to your focus, recognizing when the mind is centered and neutral toward its objects and then keeping it that way.

The pilings for the dam of mindfulness have to be driven in so that they're solid and secure with your every activity. Keep working at this no matter what you're doing. If you can train the mind so that stability is its basic stance, it won't get into mischief. It won't cause you any trouble. It won't concoct thoughts. It will be quiet. Once it's quiet and centered, it will grow more refined, probe in to penetrate itself, and know its own state of concentration from within.

As for sensory contacts, these outside things—which constantly appear only to disappear—don't interest the focused mind. This lack of interest can make cravings disband. Even when you change positions as pains arise in the body, your mind in that moment is stable, focused not on the pains but on its own stability. When you change positions, there will be physical and mental reactions as the circulation improves and pleasant feelings arise in place of the pains, but the mind won't get snagged on either the pleasure or the pain. It will stay stable, centered, and firm in its neutrality. This stability helps you to abandon the cravings that lie latent in all feelings. But if you don't keep the mind centered in advance like this, craving will create a turmoil, and the mind will start wanting to change things around so as to get this or that kind of happiness.

If you practice in this way repeatedly, hammering at this point over and over again, it's like driving pilings into the ground. The deeper you can drive them, the more immovable they'll be. That's when you'll be able to withstand sensory contacts. Otherwise the mind will start boiling over with its thought concoctions in pursuit of sights, sounds, smells, tastes, and tactile sensations. Sometimes it keeps concocting the same old senseless issues over and over again. This is because the pilings of mindfulness aren't yet firmly in place. We've been stumbling through life because we haven't practiced mindfulness continuously enough to make the mind firmly centered and neutral. So we have to make our dam of mindfulness solid and secure.

This centeredness of mind is something we should develop with every activity, with every in-and-out breath. Then we'll be able to see through our illusions, all the way into the truths of inconstancy and not-self. Otherwise the mind will stray here and there like a mischievous monkey. Yet even monkeys can be caught and trained to perform tricks. In the same way, the mind is something that can be trained, but if you don't tie it to the post of mindfulness and give it a taste of the stick, it'll be very hard to tame.

When training the mind, you shouldn't force it too much, nor can you simply let it go its habitual ways. You have to test yourself to see what gets results. If you don't get your mindfulness focused, it'll quickly run after preoccupations or waver under the impact of sense objects. When people let their minds simply drift along with the flow of things, it's because they haven't established mindfulness as a solid stance. When this is the case, they can't stop. They can't grow still. They can't be free. This is why we have to drive the pilings for our dam so that they're good and solid, keeping the mind stable and centered whether we're sitting, standing, walking, or lying down. This stability will then be able to withstand everything. Your mindfulness will stay with its foundation, just like a monkey tied to a post. It can't run off or get into mischief. It can only circle the post to which it's leashed.

Keep training the mind until it's tame enough to settle down and investigate things, for if it's still scattered about, it's of no use at all. You have to train it until it's familiar with what inner stability is like. If you waver and lack commitment in training it, the mind will get entangled with thought-concoctions, with things that arise and then pass away. You have to get it to stop. Why is it so mischievous? Why is it so scattered? Why does it keep wandering off? Get in under control! Get it to stop, settle down, and be centered!

At this stage you all have practiced enough to gain at least a taste of centered concentration. The next step is to use mindfulness to maintain it in your every activity, so that even if there are distractions, they last only for a moment and don't turn into long issues. Keep driving in the pilings until they're solid enough to withstand the impact of external objects, and until mental concoctions that go straying out from within are brought to stillness.

This training isn't really all that hard. The important point is that, whichever meditation subject you choose, you stay mindful and aware of the mind state that's centered and neutral. When the mind strays after objects, keep bringing it back to its centeredness over and over. Eventually the mind will stay firm in its stance. Mindfulness will become constant, ready to probe and investigate, *because when the mind really settles down, it gains the power to read the facts within itself clearly.* If it's not centered, it can jumble everything up to fool you, switching from this issue to that, from this role to that. But if it's centered, it can disband everything—all defilements, cravings, and attachments—on every side.

So what this practice comes down to is the effort and persistence you put into centering the mind. Once it's firm, it can withstand suffering and defilement without getting soiled or worked up, just as the pilings of a dam can withstand windstorms without budging. You have to be clearly aware of this state of mind so that you don't go liking this or hating that. This state will then become your point of departure for probing, investigating, and gaining deep insight that sees clearly all the way through—but you have to make sure that your center is continuous. Then you won't have to think about anything. Simply look right in, deeply and subtly.

The important point is that you get rid of absentmindedness and distractions. This in itself gets rid of a lot of delusion and ignorance, and leaves no opening for craving to stir up the mind and set it wandering. This is because we've established our stance in advance. Even if we lose our normal balance a little bit, we come right back to focusing on the stability of our concentration. If we keep coming back again and again, the stability of the mind with its continuous mindfulness will enable us to probe into the truths of inconstancy, stress, and not-self.

In the beginning, though, you don't have to do any probing. It's better simply to focus on the stability of your stance, for if you start probing when the mind isn't really centered and stable, you'll end up scattered. So focus on making centeredness the basic level of the mind and then start probing deeper and deeper. This will lead to insights that grow more and more telling and profound, bringing the mind to a state of freedom where it is no longer hassled by defilement.

This in itself brings you to true mastery over the sense doors. In the beginning, you can't exercise any real restraint over the eyes and ears, but once the mind becomes firmly centered, then the eyes, ears, nose, tongue, and body are automatically brought under control. If there's no mindfulness and concentration, you can't keep your eyes under control, because the mind will want to use them to look around, and it will want to use the ears to listen to all kinds of things. So instead of exercising restraint outside, at the senses, you exercise it inside, right at the mind, making the mind firmly centered and neutral at all times. Regardless of what you are doing, talking or whatever, the mind's focus stays in place. Once you can do this, you'll regard sense objects as meaningless. You won't have to take issue with things—"This is good, I like it. This is bad, I don't like it. This is pretty; that's ugly." The same holds true with the sounds you hear. You won't take issue with them. You focus instead on the neutral, uninvolved centeredness of the mind. This is the basic foundation for neutrality.

When you can do this, everything becomes neutral. When the eye sees a form, it's neutral. When the ear hears a sound, it's neutral. The mind is neutral, the sound is neutral, *everything is neutral*—because we've closed five of the six sense doors and then settled ourselves in neutrality right at the mind. This takes care of everything. Whatever the eye may see, the ear may hear, the nose may smell, the tongue may taste, or the body may touch, the mind doesn't take issue with anything at all. It stays centered, neutral, and impartial. Take just this much and give it a try.

For the next seven days I want you to make a special point of focusing mindfulness right at the mind, for this is the end of the rainy season, the period when the lotus and water lily bloom after the end of the Rains Retreat. In the Buddha's time he would have the senior monks train the new monks throughout the Rains Retreat, and then he would meet with them when the lotuses bloomed. If your stability of mind is continuous, then it too will bloom. It will bloom because the defilements haven't burned, disturbed, or provoked it. So make a special effort during the next seven days to observe and investigate the centered, neutral state of mind continuously. Of course, if you fall asleep, you fall asleep; but when you lie down to sleep, try to keep the mind centered and neutral until you doze off. When you wake up, the movements of the mind will still remain in that centered, neutral state. Give it a try, so that your mind grows calm and peaceful and disbands its defilements, cravings, sufferings—everything. Then notice whether it's beginning to bloom.

A sense of refreshment, a peace of mind undisturbed by defilement, will arise on its own. You don't have to do anything other than keep the mind stable and centered. This is your guarantee: If the mind is stable in its concentration, the defilements won't be able to burn it or mess with it. Desire won't be able to provoke it. When concentration is stable, the fires of passion, aversion, and delusion won't be able to burn it. Try to see for yourself how a stable mind withstands delusion, disbands stress, and puts out the flames. But you'll have to be earnest in practicing, in making an effort to keep mindfulness truly continuous. This isn't something to play at. You can't let yourself be weak, for if you're weak you won't be able to withstand anything. You'll simply follow the provocations of defilement and craving.

The practice is a matter of stopping so that the mind settles down and stands fast. It's a matter of not getting into mischief, of not wandering around and getting involved in issues. Try to keep the mind stable. In all your activities—eating, defecating, whatever— keep the mind centered within. If you know the state of the mind when it's centered, immovable, no longer wavering, no longer weak, then the basic level of the mind will be free and empty— empty of the things that would burn it, empty because there's no attachment. This is what enables you to ferret out the stability of the mind at every moment. It protects you from all sorts of things. All attachment to self, "me," and "them" is totally wiped out, cut away. The mind is entirely centered. If you can keep this state stable for the entire seven days, it will enable you to reach insight all on your own.

So I ask each of you to see whether or not you'll be able to make it all the way. Check to see how you're doing each day. And make sure you check things carefully. Don't let yourself be lax, sometimes stable, sometimes not. Get so that the mind is absolutely solid. Don't let yourself be weak. You have to be genuine in what you do if you want to reach the genuine extinguishing of suffering and stress. If you're not genuine, you'll weaken in the face of the provocation of wanting this or that, doing this or that, whatever, just as you've done as a slave to desire for so long.

Everyday life is where you can test yourself—so get back to the battlefield! Take a firm stance in neutrality. Then the objects that come into contact with the mind will be neutral; the mind itself will feel centered in neutrality. There will be nothing to take issue with in terms of good or bad. Everything comes to a halt in neutrality—because things in themselves aren't good or bad or "self" or whatever. It's simply that the mind has gone and made issues out of them.

So keep looking inward until you see the mind's neutrality and freedom from "self" continuously, and then you'll see how the lotus of the mind comes to bloom. If it hasn't bloomed yet, that's because it's withering in the heat of the defilements, cravings, and attachments that smolder in the mind—but eventually you'll learn to ferret them out and disband them. If you don't, the lotus will wither. Its petals will fall and rot. So make an effort to keep the lotus stable until it blooms. Don't wonder about what will happen when it blooms. Just keep it stable and make sure it isn't burned by the defilements.

THE BATTLE WITHIN

In developing mindfulness as a foundation for probing into the truth within yourself, you have to apply a level of effort and persistence appropriate to the task. This is because, as we all know, the mind is cloaked in defilements and mental fermentations. If we don't train it and force it, it'll turn weak and lax. It won't have any strength. You have to persist constantly if your probing and investigating is to penetrate to clear insight.

Clear insight doesn't come from thinking and speculating. It comes from investigating the mind while it's gathered into an adequate level of calm and stability. You look deeply into every aspect of the mind when it's neutral and calm, free from thought-fabrications and likes and dislikes. You have to work at maintaining this state and at the same time probe it deeply, because superficial knowledge isn't true knowledge. As long as you haven't probed deeply into the mind, you don't really know anything. The mind may be calm on an external level, but your reading of the wanderings of the mind under the influence of defilement, craving, and attachment isn't yet clear.

So you have to peer into yourself until you reach a level of awareness that can maintain its balance and let you contemplate your way to sharper understanding. If you don't contemplate so as to give rise to true knowledge, your mindfulness will stay on the surface.

The same principle holds when you're contemplating the body. You have to probe deeply into how the body is repulsive and composed of physical elements. This is what it means to *read* the body, to understand it. By exploring yourself in all your activities, you prevent your mind from straying off the path. You stay focused on seeing how mindfulness burns away the defilements as they arise— which is very delicate work.

Being heedful and not letting yourself get distracted by outside things is what will make the practice go smoothly. It will enable you to examine the germs in the mind in a skillful way so that you can eliminate the subtlest ones: ignorance and delusion. Normally, we aren't fully aware of even the blatant germs, but now that the blatant ones are inactivated because of the mind's solid focus, we can look deeper and catch sight of the deceits of craving and defilements as they move into action. If we watch them and get to know them, we are in a good position to abandon them as soon as they wander in search of enticing sights, sounds, smells, and flavors. Whether they're looking for good physical flavors—bodily pleasure—or good mental flavors, we have to study them from all sides, even though they're not easy to know because of our desire for physical pleasure.

Our desires for happiness—and all our perceptions, thought-fabrications, and states of consciousness imbued with pleasurable feelings—are nothing but desires for illusions, for things that engross and distract us. As a result, it isn't easy for us to understand much of anything at all.

These are subtle matters, and they all come under the term "sensual craving"—the desire, lust, and love that provoke the mind into wandering out in search of the enjoyment it remembers from past sights, sounds, smells, tastes, and tactile sensations. Even though these things may have happened long ago, our perceptions bring them back to deceive us with ideas of their being good or bad. Once we latch onto them, they defile and unsettle the mind.

So it isn't easy to examine and understand the various germs within the mind. The external things we're able to know and let go of are only the minor players. The important ones have gathered together to take charge in the mind and won't budge no matter how hard you try to chase them out. They're stubborn and determined to stay in charge. If you take them on when your mindfulness and discernment aren't equal to the fight, you'll end up losing your inner calm.

So you have to make sure that you don't push the practice too much, and at the same time don't let it grow too slack. Find the Middle Way that's just right. While you're practicing in this way, you'll be able to observe what the mind is like when it has mindfulness and discernment in charge, and then you make the effort to *maintain* that state and keep it constant. That's when the mind will have the opportunity to stop and be still, to be stable and centered for long periods until it's used to being that way.

Now, there are some areas where we have to force the mind and be strict with it. If we're weak and lax, and have long given in to our own wants, there's no way we can succeed. If we keep giving in, that will become even more of a habit. So you have to use force— the force of your will and the force of your mindfulness and discernment. Even if you get to the point where you have to put your life on the line, you've got to be willing. When the time comes for you really to be serious, you've got to hold out until you come out winning. If you don't win, don't give up. Make a vow as a way of forcing yourself to overcome your stubborn desires for physical pleasure that tempt you and lead you astray.

If you're weak and settle for whatever pleasure comes in the immediate present, then when desire comes in, you'll fall for it. If you give in to your wants often, it'll become habitual, for defilement is always looking for the chance to tempt you, to incite you. When we try to give up an addiction—to coffee, cigarettes, or meat—it's hard because craving always comes to tempt us. "Just take a little," it says. "Just a taste. It doesn't matter." Craving knows how to fool us, the way a fish is fooled into getting caught on a hook by the bait surrounding the hook, screwing up its courage to take just a little, and then a little more, and then a little more until it gets snagged. The demons of defilement have us surrounded on all sides. Once we fall for their delicious flavors, we're sure to get snagged on the hook. No matter how much we struggle and squirm, we can't get free.

You have to realize that gaining victory over your enemies— the cravings and defilements in the heart—is no small matter, no casual affair. You can't let yourself be weak or lax, but you also have to gauge your strength. Defilements and cravings have the power of demons, so you may have to figure out how best to apply your efforts to overcome and destroy them. You don't have to battle to the brink of death in every area. With some things—such as giving up addictions—you can mount a full-scale campaign and come out winning without killing yourself in the process. But with other things, more subtle and deep, you have to be more perceptive. You have to figure out how to overcome them over the long haul, by digging up their roots so that they gradually weaken to the point where your mindfulness and discernment can overwhelm them. If there are areas where you're losing out, take stock of yourself with sensitivity and figure out why. Otherwise, you'll keep losing out, for when the defilements really want something, they trample over your mindfulness and discernment in their determination to get it. "That's what I want. I don't care what anyone says." They really are that stubborn! So it's no small matter, figuring out how to bring them under control. It's like running into an enemy or facing a wild beast rushing to devour you. What are you going to do?

When the defilements arise right before your eyes, you have to be wary. Suppose you're perfectly aware, and all of a sudden they spring up and confront you. What kind of mindfulness and discernment are you going to use to disband them? "These are the hordes of Māra, come to burn and eat me. How am I going to get rid of them?" Can you tell yourself that? In other words, can you find a skillful way to contemplate them so as to destroy them right then and there?

We have to find such a way, regardless of whether we're being confronted with physical or mental pain or pleasure. Actually, pleasure is more treacherous than pain because it's harder to fathom and easier to fall for. As for pain, no one falls for it because it's so uncomfortable. So how are we going to contemplate so as to let go of *both* the pleasure *and* the pain? This is the problem we face at every moment. It's not that when we practice we accept only the pleasure and stop when we run into pain. That's not the case at all. We have to learn how to read *both* sides, to see that pain is inconstant and stressful and that pleasure is inconstant and stressful, too. We have to penetrate clear through these things. Otherwise we'll be deluded by deceitful, pleasure-seeking cravings. Our every activity—sitting, standing, walking, lying down—is really for the sake of pleasure, isn't it?

This is why there are so many, many ways in which we're deluded by pleasure. Whatever we do, we do for the sake of pleasure without realizing how deeply we've mired ourselves in suffering and stress. When we contemplate inconstancy, stress, and not-selfness, we don't get anywhere in our contemplation because we haven't seen through pleasure. We still think that it's a good thing. We have to probe into the fact that there's no real ease to physical or mental pleasure. It's all stress. When you can see it from this angle, that's when you'll come to understand inconstancy.

Then once the mind isn't focused on always wanting pleasure, your stresses and pains will lighten. You'll be able to see them as something common and normal. You'll see that however hard you try to change the pain to find ease, there's no ease to be found. Then you won't be overly concerned with trying to change the pain, for you'll see that there's no pleasure or ease in the aggregates, that they give us nothing but stress and pain. We know this from the Buddha's teachings that we chant every day: "Form is stressful, feeling, perception, thought-fabrications, and consciousness are all stressful." *The problem is that we haven't investigated into the truth of our own form, feelings, perceptions, thought-fabrications, and consciousness.* Our insight doesn't penetrate because we haven't looked from the angle of true knowing. And so we get deluded here and lost there in our search for pleasure, finding nothing but pain and yet mistaking it for pleasure. This shows that we still haven't opened our ears and eyes; we still don't know the truth. Once we do know the truth, though, the mind will be inclined to grow still and calm rather than to wander off in pursuit of pleasure. Once it realizes there's no real pleasure to be found in that way, it settles down and grows still.

All the cravings that provoke and unsettle the mind come down to nothing but the desire for pleasure. So we have to see that the aggregates have no pleasure to offer, that they're stressful by their very nature. They're not us or ours. Take them apart and have a good look at them, starting with the body. Analyze the body down to its elements so that the mind won't keep latching on to it as "me" or "mine." You have to do this over and over again until you really understand.

Every day we chant the *Recollection while Using the Requisites*—food, clothing, shelter, and medicine—to gain real understanding. If we don't do this every day, we forget and get deluded into loving the body and worrying about it, believing it's "my body," "my self." No matter how much we keep latching onto it over and over, we have trouble realizing what we're doing, even though we have access to the Buddha's teachings and they explain everything completely. Or we may contemplate to some extent but not see things clearly. We see only in a vague, blurry way and then flit off, oblivious, without probing enough to see all the way through. We do that because the mind isn't firmly centered. It isn't still. It keeps wandering off to find things to think about and gets itself all agitated. So it doesn't get to know anything at all. All it knows are a few little perceptions. This is the way it's been for who knows how many years now. It's as if our vision has been clouded by spots that we haven't yet removed from our eyes.

Those who aren't interested in exploring, who make no effort to get to the facts, don't wonder about anything at all. They're free from doubt, all right, but it's because delusion has smothered all doubt. If we start exploring and contemplating, we begin to wonder about things: "What's this? What does it mean? How should I deal with it?" These are questions that lead us to explore. If we don't explore, it's because we don't have any intelligence. Or we may gain a few little insights, but we let them pass so that we never explore deeply into the basic principles of the practice. What little we *do* know doesn't go anywhere, doesn't penetrate to the Noble Truths, because our mindfulness and discernment run out of strength. Our persistence isn't resilient enough, isn't brave enough. We don't dare look deep inside ourselves.

To trust our own estimates of how far is enough in the practice is to lie to ourselves. It keeps us from gaining release from suffering and stress. If you happen to come up with a few insights, don't go bragging about them or you'll end up deceiving yourself in countless ways. Those who really know, even when they *have* attained the various stages of insight, are heedful to keep on exploring. They don't get stuck at this stage or that. Even when their insights are correct they don't stop right there and start bragging, for that's the way of a fool.

Intelligent people, even though they see things clearly, always keep an eye out for the enemies lying in wait for them on the deeper, more subtle levels ahead. They have to keep penetrating further. They have no sense that this or that level is plenty enough—for how can it be enough? The defilements are still burning away, so how can you brag? Even though your knowledge may be true, how can you be complacent when your mind has yet to establish a foundation for itself?

As you investigate with mindfulness and discernment, complacency is the major problem. You have to be heedful in the practice if
you want to keep up with the fact that life is ebbing away, ebbing
with every moment. And how should you live so that you can be said
to be heedful? This is an extremely important question, for if you're
not alive to it, then no matter how many days or months you practice meditation or restraint of the senses, it's simply a temporary
exercise. When you're done, you get back to your same old turmoil.

And watch your mouth. You'll have trouble not bragging, for
the defilements will provoke you into speaking. They want to
speak, they want to brag, they won't let you stay silent.

If you force yourself in the practice without understanding its
true aims, you end up deceiving yourself and go around telling people, "I practiced in silence for so many days, so many months."
This is deceiving yourself and others as well. The truth of the matter is that without realizing it you're still a slave to stupidity, obey-
ing the many levels of defilement and craving within yourself. If
someone praises you, you really prick up your ears, wag your tail,
and, instead of explaining the harm of the defilements and craving
you find within yourself, you brag.

So the practice of the Dhamma isn't something you can just
muddle your way through. You have to do it with your intelligence fully alert. When you contemplate in a circumspect way,
you'll see that there's nothing worth getting engrossed in, that
everything—both inside and out—is nothing but an illusion. It's
like being adrift, alone in the middle of the ocean with no island or
shore in sight. Can you afford just to sit back and relax, to make a
temporary effort and then brag about it? Of course not! As your
investigation penetrates inward to ever more subtle levels of the
mind, you have to become more and more calm and reserved, in

the same way that people become more and more circumspect as they grow up. Your mindfulness and discernment have to keep maturing in order to understand what's right and wrong, true and false, in whatever arises: That's what will enable you to let go and gain release. And that's what will make your life in the true practice of the Dhamma go smoothly. Otherwise, you'll fool yourself into boasting about how many years you've practiced meditation and will eventually find yourself worse than before, with defilement flaring up in a big way. If this is the way you go, you'll end up tumbling head over heels into fire—for when you raise your head in pride, you run into the flames already burning within yourself.

To practice means to use the fire of mindfulness and discernment as a counter-fire to put out the blaze of the defilements, because the heart and mind are aflame with defilement, and when we use the fire of mindfulness and discernment to put out the fire of defilement, the mind can cool down. Do this by being increasingly honest with yourself, without leaving an opening for defilement and craving to insinuate their way into control. You have to be alert. Circumspect. Wise to them. Don't fall for them! If you fall for whatever rationale they come up with, it means that your mindfulness and discernment are still weak. They'll lead you away by the nose, burning you with their fire right before your very eyes, and yet you'll still open your mouth to brag!

So turn around and take stock of everything within yourself. Take stock of every aspect, because everything right and wrong, true and false, lies within you. You can't find them outside. The damaging things people say about you are nothing compared to the damage caused inside you when defilement burns you, when your feeling of "me" and "mine" raises its head.

If you don't honestly come to your senses, there's no way your practice of the Dhamma can gain you release from the great mass of suffering and stress. You may be able to gain a little knowledge and let go of a few things, but the roots of the problem will still lie buried deep down. So you have to dig them out. You can't relax after little bouts of emptiness and equanimity. That won't accomplish anything. The defilements and mental fermentations lie deep in the personality, so you have to use mindfulness and discernment to penetrate deep down to make a precise and thorough examination. Only then will you get results. Otherwise, if you stay only on the surface level, you can practice until your body lies rotting in its coffin but you won't have changed any of your basic habits.

Those who are scrupulous by nature, who know how to contemplate their own flaws, will keep on the alert for any signs of pride within themselves. They'll try to control and destroy conceit on every side and won't allow it to swell. The methods we need to use in the practice for examining and destroying the germs within the mind aren't easy to master. For those who don't contemplate themselves thoroughly, the practice may actually increase their pride, their bragging, their desire to teach others. But if we turn within and discern the deceits and conceits of the self, a profound feeling of disenchantment and dismay arises, causing us to pity ourselves for how much stupidity we carry around, for how much we've deluded ourselves all along, and for how much effort we'll still need to apply in the practice.

So however great the pain and anguish, however many tears bathe your cheeks, persevere! The practice isn't simply a matter of looking for mental and physical pleasure. "Let tears bathe my cheeks, but I'll keep on with my striving at the holy life as long as I live!" That's the way it has to be! Don't quit at the first small difficulty with the thought "It's a waste of time. I'd do better to follow my cravings and defilements." You can't think like that! You have to take the exact opposite stance: "When they tempt me to grab this, take a lot of that—I won't! However fantastic the object may be, I won't take the bait." Make a firm declaration! This is the only way to get results. Otherwise, you'll never work yourself free, for the defilements have all sorts of tricks up their sleeves. If you get wise to one trick, they simply change to another, and then another.

If we're not observant enough to see how the defilements have deceived us in all sorts of ways, we won't come to know the truth within ourselves. Other people may fool us now and then, but the defilements fool us always. We fall for them and follow them hook, line, and sinker. Our trust in the Lord Buddha is nothing compared to our trust in them. We're disciples of the demons of craving, letting them lead us ever deeper into their jungle.

If we don't see this for ourselves, we're lost in that jungle charnel ground where the demons keep roasting us to make us squirm with desires and every form of distress. Even if you stay in a place with few disturbances, like this Dhamma center, these demons still manage to tempt you. Just notice how the saliva flows when you come across anything delicious! *So you have to decide to be either a warrior or a loser.* The practice requires that you do battle with defilements and cravings. Always be on your guard, whatever the approach they take to seduce and deceive you. Other people can't induce you to follow them, but the demons of your own defilements can because you trust them and agree to be their slave. You have to contemplate carefully so that you're no longer enslaved to them and can reach total freedom. Develop your mindfulness and discernment, gain clear insight, and then let go until suffering and stress disband in every way!

STOP, LOOK, AND LET GO

We discuss the practice for the sake of reminding ourselves to keep getting better and better results. If we don't discuss these matters, we tend to weaken in the face of thought-fabrications, as we're so accustomed to doing. Training the mind to be quiet requires a lot of circumspection, because the mind is basically unruly and contrary. It won't easily stay under the supervision of mindfulness and discernment. So we have to develop the knowledge that will keep it under control in an appropriate way.

To get the mind to stay under the control of mindfulness and discernment, we have to stop and watch it, stop and know it. How the mind is fashioned and how it can be sensed are hard for us to understand, because the mind likes to wander around according to its thought-fabrications. If we want to sense it in and of itself, we have to subject it to a lot of training. Learning to supervise it, getting it under the control of mindfulness and discernment, takes time.

And you have to use your powers of observation and evaluation. If you don't keep on observing and evaluating as part of your practice, the mind will quickly slip away and wander wherever its preoccupations lead it. Its travels will bring you nothing but suffering and stress. You'll gain nothing good from it. The mind simply goes out looking for trouble. Regardless of whether you like things or dislike them, you grasp them and turn them into suffering. The eyes, the ears, and the other sense doors are bridges that the mind crosses the moment you see sights, hear sounds, or notice other sensory contact. How can you exercise care and restraint over the sense doors so that they lie under the power of your mindfulness? You have to observe the results that come from looking and listening in a *mindful* way. If you don't use your powers of observation and evaluation, you tend to latch onto the sensations of what you've seen or heard. Then you label them, fabricate things out of them, and latch onto those things with love and hate until your mind is in a turmoil.

Observe the sensations that arise at each of the sense doors to see that they're just sensations happening, pure and simple. It's not that *we* sense these things. The eye sees forms. It's not us that's seeing them. There's simply the seeing of forms by means of eye-consciousness, pure and simple. At that point, there's not yet any labeling of the sight as good or bad. There's not yet any thought-fabrication following on the sensation of contact. We simply watch the simple sensation and then stop right there, to see the characteristics of the sensation as it passes away or as it's replaced by a new sensation. We keep watching the passing away of sensations, keep watching until we see that this is simply the nature of the eyes and ears: to register sensations. That way we don't latch onto them to the point where we give rise to suffering and stress the way we used to.

If we don't watch carefully and see this natural arising and passing away, we tend to mix everything up. For instance, when the eye sees, we assume that *we* see. The things we see either please us or don't, give pleasure or pain, and we latch onto them to the point where they defile the mind. If you're not careful and observant, everything coming in through the sense doors develops into mental fabrication and affects the mind. This gives rise to suffering, because whenever the eye sees sights and the ear hears sounds, the power of your attachments leaves you unaware of how these things just arise, stay, and pass away.

How can we begin to disentangle ourselves from these things so that we don't stay attached? How should we be mindful in our looking and listening? We have to keep observing the mind to see that, when there's mindfulness at the moment of seeing a sight, the mind can stay neutral. It doesn't have to be pleased or displeased. If we're mindful when the ear hears sounds, we can make sure that the mind isn't pleased or displeased with the sounds. The same holds true with smells, tastes, tactile sensations, and ideas. We have to focus on the mind, which is the factor in charge, the stem point. *If we exercise restraint over the mind, then that, in and of itself, keeps all the sense doors restrained.* The eye will be restrained in seeing sights: Involvement in seeing will get shorter. When the ear hears sounds, the mind can stay neutral as it focuses on being alert to the arising and passing away of sounds or on the sensation of sound as it constantly comes and goes. Otherwise, if you don't develop this approach, everything gets thrown into confusion. The mind has nothing but attachments and feelings of self, giving rise to all sorts of suffering simply from its lack of restraint. This is something we've all experienced.

The virtue of restraining the senses *(indriya-saṁvara-sīla)* is a very refined level of virtue—and a very useful one, too. If you develop this level of virtue, the other levels become purer. If you don't exercise restraint over the eyes, ears, nose, and so forth, then your five, eight, or ten precepts can't stay firm. They'll be easily soiled. If the eye, which is the bridge, isn't restrained, then it focuses its attention outside. And when this happens, overstepping your precepts becomes the easiest thing in the world. If you allow the mind to get accustomed to running after outside preoccupations, everything gets thrown into a turmoil. The turmoil starts there in the mind, and then it spreads out to your words and deeds, so that you speak and act in wrong ways.

If we try to observe the precepts without restraining the senses, our precepts can't become pure. This is because we aren't careful about how we look and listen, so we can't see how desire, craving, and defilement arise at the moment the eye sees sights or the ear hears sounds. *This lack of restraint is what puts holes in our precepts.* We create issues outside, and this soils our words and deeds. Restraint of the senses is thus a level of virtue that seals off the leaks in the mind. If you develop this level of virtue, your words and deeds will be beautiful and admirable—just like monks who are strict in their restraint of the senses, who don't gaze far away, who don't look at things that are enemies to the mind, who aren't addicted to the flavors of contact by means of the eye, ear, nose, tongue, body, and mind, and who are observant of the passing away of physical and mental phenomena so that their minds aren't thrown into a turmoil because of their likes and dislikes.

For the most part, we aren't interested in exercising restraint, so we fall victim to sensual pleasures. We let ourselves get pleased and displeased with sights, sounds, smells, tastes, and tactile sensations; and so the mind gets defiled when, in its delusion, it falls for the savor of these things. No matter how deluded we get, we don't realize what's happening because the savor of these pleasures leads us to want more. Our discernment hasn't yet seen the drawbacks of these things. *To let go of anything, you first have to see its drawbacks.* If you simply tell yourself to let go, let go, let go, you can't really let go. You have to see the drawbacks of the things you're holding on to, and then you'll let go automatically—as when you grab hold of fire and realize how hot it is, you'll automatically let go and never dare touch it again. We haven't yet realized the heat of sensual passions, which is why we still like them so much. Even though every attachment is stressful by its very nature, we see it as good. No matter what comes our way, we keep latching on. This has become our second nature. We're not aware that we're grabbing hold of fire and so we keep wanting more of it. This is why the mind never wearies of its clinging attachments.

When we can't see the drawbacks of sensual passions, there's no way we can see the drawbacks of more subtle things that lie deeper still, like our sense of self. We're still lured by external baits by way of the eye and ear, and yet we're not aware of what's happening. These things are like the sugar coating on a pill of poison. We find the pill sweet. We swallow the poison, which nourishes cravings and defilements that are so painful and searing, yet we don't see them as painful. We're still relishing the sugar. We want more. This is because the mind has never grown weary of sensuality, hasn't developed any sense of renunciation, any desire to be free. It still likes to soak in sensuality. If it gains sensual pleasure, it's satisfied. If it doesn't, it gets angry and resentful.

Even these external lures still delude us. If we get what we want, we're happy. If we don't, we're thrown into a turmoil. If we don't get enough of these lures, we go around complaining that other people don't sympathize with us, don't care about us. We keep wanting to get these things, with no sense of enough—like worms that feel such relish for foul and smelly things and have no sense of disgust. The savor of sensual passion excites the hearts of all beings so that they want more. The Noble Ones feel disgust and don't want to go near it, but ordinary beings go right for it and gobble up their fill. The Buddha compared people like this to worms that relish filth, or to a snake that's fallen into a cesspool, so covered with excrement that you can't find any part to grab hold of to get it out without soiling yourself. The Buddha liked to make comparisons like this so that we'll come to our senses.

The Buddha had a whole long list of comparisons for the drawbacks of sensual pleasures. If you want to know what they are, look in a good anthology of the suttas. Some of the Buddha's teachings are attractive and appealing, but others are really castigating. We meditators should take an interest in reading his teachings and reflecting on them, so that we don't misunderstand things. Dhamma that pokes at our sore points goes against the grain with all of us, because we don't like criticism. We don't like being reprimanded. We want nothing but praise and admiration, to the point where we swell with pride. But people with real mindfulness and discernment don't want any of that. They want to hear helpful criticism, helpful reprimands. *This is what it means to have discernment and intelligence. You know how to take criticism in an intelligent way.*

When you read the Buddha's teachings, you should reflect on them. The Buddha castigates his disciples more than he praises them. Is our attitude in line with his? We like to hear praise. If people criticize us, we get angry and accuse them of having bad motives. This is really stupid and sad. We get teachings that are meant to help us, but we don't use them to reflect on ourselves. Instead, we criticize the teaching as being too negative, too harsh. As a result, we don't get any use out of well-meaning criticisms. But people with mindfulness and discernment feel just the other way around. They realize that they benefit from their teachers' criticisms more than from anything else.

Children have no appreciation for the teachers who have been strict with them because they hate strict treatment. But as they become more intelligent and mature, they begin to realize that strict treatment can be an excellent way of building character, of making them come to their senses. The old saying "If you love your ox you can't let it roam wild; if you love your child you have to spank it" reminds us not to cater to our children's whims, or else they'll become careless and irresponsible. If we're strict with them and scold them when they do wrong, they'll develop a greater sense of responsibility.

This is why people who are intelligent and discerning prefer criticism to praise. Stupid people prefer praise to criticism. As soon as you criticize them, they get *so* angry. They don't realize the great value of criticism. Suppose someone criticizes us when we do wrong: the wrong we're doing is unskillful and causes suffering. If we're warned against doing something unskillful, that's greatly to our benefit. It's as if that person has pulled us out of suffering, out of a fire, out of hell.

But stupid people will attack the person who gives them a well-intentioned warning. If they were intelligent, they'd thank that person for helping them come to their senses. They'd take the warning to heart and never forget it. If you don't feel this way about criticism, you'll never outgrow your old habits. You'll stick stubbornly to your old ways, more concerned with winning over others than with taming your own rebelliousness. If you can't tame your rebelliousness, then the more you're taught, the more you go out of control— and the more you simply end up burning yourself. You take valuable teachings and use them to harm yourself. This is why we have to listen well to criticism, so that we can get the most benefit from it.

Think of how harmful defilement, craving, and attachment can be! We're so full of our sense of self. What can we do to weaken it? We have to focus on our own minds in a way that gives results, that doesn't defile it, that doesn't stir it up into a turmoil. We have to use our own intelligence—our own mindfulness and discernment—to keep looking inward at all times. No one else can do our looking for us. We're the ones who have to know ourselves in an all-around way.

Think of this practice of ridding ourselves of defilements as digging into a big termites' nest to get at a vicious animal—like a snake—hiding inside. You have to use the sharpest possible picks and shovels to reach the snake. In the same way, our sense of self lies deep. We have to use mindfulness and discernment, sharp as picks and shovels, to penetrate into it. Wherever there's a sense of self, try digging in to catch it. Turn it over and look at its face, to see where exactly it's your self. Try examining your body, or feelings, perceptions, thought-fabrications, and consciousness—all the things you're so attached to and are unwilling to let go. How can you examine them so that you'll know them? Only through seeing the inconstancy of forms, feelings, perceptions, thought-fabrications, and consciousness. If you don't understand this, there's no way you can let go of these things, for you'll keep on misperceiving them, thinking that they're constant, easeful, and self.

This is an important point. Don't pass over it casually. The affairs of inconstancy, stress, and not-selfness are deep and refined. As we start from the outer levels and work our way in, our contemplation must grow deeper and more refined. Don't settle for knowing inconstancy, stress, and not-selfness only on a superficial level, for that'll have no impact on the roots of your delusion and foolishness. Find out which ways of contemplating get results in producing knowledge of inconstancy, stress, and not-selfness with genuine mindfulness and discernment. If you really know with mindfulness and discernment, the mind has to develop a sense of *saṁvega,* of chastened dismay over the inconstancy, stressfulness, and not-selfness of physical and mental phenomena, of the five aggregates—in other words, of our body and mind. It'll then unravel its attachments. But if our knowledge isn't yet true, we'll keep on holding on blindly, trying to make these things constant, easeful, and self.

I ask that you all contemplate so you can come to know these matters for what they are. The whole reason we're trying to quiet our minds or practice meditation is nothing other than this: to see the inconstancy, stress, and not-selfness of the aggregates, the properties—earth, water, fire, wind, space, and consciousness—or the sense media: eyes, ears, nose, tongue, body, and intellect. We're not practicing simply for the ease and pleasure that come when the mind is still. We have to observe and evaluate things so as to see them clearly *in a way that allows us to let them go.* The mind will then be empty of any sense of self. Even if you can experience this emptiness only momentarily, it's still very worthwhile. Keep your awareness of that experience in mind as capital for continued strength in the practice—better than wandering off to be aware of other things.

When we keep on training the mind day after day, as we're doing here, we find that when we go to sleep and then wake up in the morning, our awareness has become continuous—more and more continuous, to the point where the mind doesn't go wandering off the way it used to. It stays more and more with the body in the present. Whatever arises, we can investigate it to see if any part of it is constant or stable. Regardless of whether it's a physical phenomenon or a mental phenomenon, is any part of it constant or stable? When we see that there's nothing constant or stable to these things, that they keep on changing relentlessly, we'll realize that this inconstancy is inherently stressful—and that within this inconstancy that's inherently stressful, there's no *self* anywhere at all.

You have to investigate things clearly in this way. *It's not that inconstancy is one thing, stress another, and not-self still another. That's not the case at all. You have to investigate to see clearly that they're all aspects of the same thing.* If you don't see this clearly with your own mindfulness and discernment, your knowledge isn't true. Even though you may be able to explain things correctly, the mind still doesn't know. It keeps its eyes closed and stays in the dark. When your knowledge is true, there has to be a sense of dispassion, of letting go. The mind will be able to abandon its attachments.

Then watch the mind at that moment. You'll see that it's empty.

Look at your mind right now. When it's at a state of normalcy, free from any turmoil, it's empty on one level. When you turn to observe the mind at a state of normalcy, when it's not latching onto anything, it's free from any sense of self. There's simply awareness, pure and simple, without any labels of "me" or "mine." Notice how the mind is empty right now because it doesn't have any attachments to "me" or "mine."

If you don't understand this point, you won't be able to find the deeper levels of emptiness—or you may go and make it empty in other ways, all of which are off the mark. *The emptiness we're looking for comes from letting things go through seeing their inconstancy, stressfulness, and not-selfness.* And then you have to keep hammering away at this point, over and over again. There's no need to pay attention to any other matters, for the more things you take on, the more the mind is thrown into a turmoil. Focus on one matter, one thing, and keep observing it until it's clear to the mind. The moment it's clear is when the mind will be able to loosen its grip. It'll be able to let go. To be empty. Even just this is enough for extinguishing the suffering and stress of your day-to-day life. You don't have to go reading or studying a lot of things. Simply study the mind from this angle—its arising, remaining, and passing away. Observe this until it's clear, and the mind will become firmly centered in this awareness. When it's aware, it lets go. It'll then be empty.

So this all boils down to one point: Try to be intent on observing and evaluating the mind carefully, and it will become empty in the easiest possible way. I hope that this simple point will help you see the truth correctly within your mind, and that you'll reap the benefits with each and every moment

ALL THINGS ARE UNWORTHY OF ATTACHMENT

It's very beneficial that we have practiced the Dhamma by contemplating ourselves step by step and have—to some extent—come to know the truth. This is because each person has to find the truth within: the truths of stress, its cause, and the path leading to its disbanding. If we don't know these things, we fall into the same suffering as the rest of the world. We may have come to live in a Dhamma center, yet if we don't know these truths we don't benefit from staying here. The only way we differ from living at home is that we're observing the precepts. If we don't want to be deluded in our practice, these truths are things we have to know. Otherwise, we get deluded into looking for our fun in the stresses and sufferings offered by the world.

Our practice is to contemplate until we understand stress and its causes, namely, the defilements that have so much power and authority over the heart and mind. It's only because of this practice that we can disband these defilements and their resultant stress every day and at all times. This is something really marvelous. Those who don't practice don't have a clue, even though they live enveloped by defilements and stress. They simply get led around by the nose into more and more suffering, and yet none of them realizes what's going on. If we don't make contact with the Dhamma, if we don't practice, we go through birth and death simply to create *kamma* with one another and to keep whirling around in suffering and stress.

We have to contemplate stress until we *see* it. That's when we'll drop our heedlessness and try to disband stress or to gain release from it. The practice is thus a matter of struggling to gain victory over stress and suffering, and with better and better results. Whatever mistakes we make in whatever way, we try not to repeat them. And we have to contemplate the harm and suffering caused by the more subtle defilements, cravings, and attachments within us. This is why we have to probe into the deeper, more profound parts of the heart—for if we stay only on the superficial levels of emptiness in the mind, we won't gain any profound knowledge at all.

So we train the mind to be mindful and firmly centered, and to focus on looking within, knowing within. Don't let it get distracted outside. When it focuses within, it will come to know the truth: the truth of stress and of the causes of stress—defilement, craving, and attachment—as they arise. It will see what they're like and how to probe inward to disband them

When all is said and done, the practice comes down to one issue, because it focuses exclusively on one thing: stress together with its cause. This is the central issue in human life—even animals are in the same predicament—but our ignorance deludes us into latching onto all kinds of things. This is because of our misunderstandings or wrong views. If we gain Right View, we see things correctly. Whenever we see stress, we see its truth. When we see the cause of stress, we see its truth. We see because we've focused on it. *If you don't focus on stress, you won't know it; but as soon as you focus on it, you will.* It's because the mind hasn't focused here that it wanders out oblivious, chasing after its preoccupations.

When we try to focus the mind, it struggles and resists because it's used to wandering. But if we keep focusing frequently, we'll get a sense of how to bring the mind under control. Then the task becomes easier. The mind no longer struggles to chase after its pre-occupations as it did before. No matter how much it resists when we start training it, eventually we're sure to bring it under our control, getting it to settle down and be still. If it doesn't settle down, you have to contemplate it. You have to show it that you mean business. This is because defilement and craving are very strong. You can't be weak when dealing with them. You have to be brave, to have a fight-to-the-death attitude, and to sustain your efforts. If you're concerned only with finding comfort and pleasure, you'll never gain release.

Their power envelops everything in our character, making it very difficult for us to find out the truth about ourselves. What we do know is just a smattering, and so we play truant, abandoning the task, and end up thinking that the practice of the Dhamma isn't important. Rather than be strict with ourselves, we get involved in all kinds of things, for that's the path the defilements keep pointing out to us. We grope along weakly, giving in to the defilements and taking their bait. When they complain about the slightest discomfort, we quickly pander to them and take the bait again. It's because we're so addicted to the bait that we don't appreciate either the power of craving—as it wanders out after sights, sounds, and so forth—or its harm in making us scattered and restless, unable to stay still and contemplate ourselves. It's always finding things for us to do, to think about, making us suffer, and yet we remain blind to the fact.

Now that we've come to practice the Dhamma, we begin to have a sense of what's going on. Whoever practices without being complacent will find that defilement and stress grow lighter and lighter, step by step. The areas where we used to be defeated, we now come out victorious. Where we used to be burned by the defilements, we now have the mindfulness and discernment to burn *them* instead. Only when we stop groping around and really come to our senses will we realize the benefits of the Dhamma, the importance of the practice. Then there is no way that we can abandon the practice, for something inside us keeps forcing us to stay with it. If we don't practice to disband defilement, stress will keep piling up. This is why we have to stay with the practice to our last breath.

You have to be firm and not let yourself be led astray. Those who are mindful and discerning will naturally act in this way. Those who aren't will keep on following their defilements, ending up back where they were before they started practicing to gain release from stress. They may keep on practicing, but it's hard to tell what they're practicing for—mostly for more stress. This shows that they're still groping—and when they grope this way, they start criticizing the practice as useless and bad.

If you submit readily to defilement and craving, there's no way you can practice. It's like paddling a boat against the stream—you have to use strength if you want to make any headway. It's not easy to go against the stream of the defilements, because they are always ready to pull you downstream. If you aren't mindful and discerning, if you don't use the Lord Buddha's Dhamma to examine yourself, your strength will fail you. If you have only a little mindfulness and discernment in the face of a lot of defilements, they'll make you vacillate. And if you're living with sweet-talking sycophants, you'll go even further off the path. You'll get involved with all sorts of extraneous issues and become oblivious to the practice.

To practice the Dhamma, then, is to go *against* the flow, to go upstream against suffering and stress. If you don't contemplate stress, your practice will go nowhere. Stress is where you start, and then you try to trace out its root cause. You have to use your discernment to track down exactly where stress originates, for stress is a result. Once you see the result, you have to track down the cause. Those who are mindful and discerning are never complacent. Whenever stress arises they're sure to search out its causes so that they can eliminate them. This sort of investigation can proceed on many levels, from the coarse to the refined, and requires that you seek advice so that you don't stumble. You might think you can figure it all out in your head—but that won't work at all!

The basic Dhamma principles that the Lord Buddha proclaimed for us to use in our contemplation are many, but there's no need to learn them all. Just focusing on some of the more important ones, such as the five aggregates or name and form, will be very useful. But you need to keep making a thorough, all-around examination, not just an occasional probe, so that a feeling of dispassion and disengagement arises and loosens the grip of desire. If you use mindfulness to keep constant and close supervision over the senses, that mindfulness will become stronger than your tendency to drift off. Regardless of what you're doing, saying, or thinking, be on the lookout for whatever will make you slip, for if you're tenacious in sustaining mindfulness, that's how all your stresses and sufferings can be disbanded.

So keep at this. If you fall down a hundred times, get back up a hundred times and resume your stance. The reason mindfulness and discernment are slow to develop is because you're not really sensitive to yourself. The greater your sensitivity, the stronger your mindfulness and discernment will become. As the Lord Buddha said, *"Bhāvitā bahulīkatā"*—which means, "Develop and maximize"—in other words, make the most of your mindfulness.

The way your practice has developed through contemplating and supervising the mind in daily life has already shown some rewards, so keep stepping up your efforts. Don't let yourself grow weak or lax. Now that you finally have this opportunity, can you afford to be complacent? Your life is steadily ebbing away, so you have to compensate by building up more and more mindfulness and discernment until you become mature in the Dhamma. Otherwise, your defilements will remain many and your discernment crude. The older you are, the more watchful you must be—for we know what happens to old people everywhere.

So seize the moment to develop the faculties of conviction, persistence, mindfulness, concentration, and discernment in a balanced way. Keep contemplating and probing, and you'll protect yourself from wandering out after the world. No matter who tempts you to go with them, you won't follow, because you'll no longer believe anyone else or get lured by the baits of the world— *for the baits of the world are poison, and the Dhamma has to be the refuge and light of your life.* Once you have this degree of conviction in yourself, you can't help but stride forward without slipping back; but if you waver and wander, unsure of whether to keep practicing the Dhamma, watch out: You're sure to get pulled over the cliff and into the pit of fire.

If you aren't free within yourself, you get pulled from all sides because the world is full of things that keep pulling at you. But those who have the intelligence not to be gullible will see the stress and harm of those things distinctly for themselves. They won't head for anything low, and they won't have to keep suffering in the world. They feel dispassion. They lose their taste for all the various baits and lures the world has to offer.

The practice of the Dhamma allows us to shake off whatever attractive things used to delude us into holding on. Realize that it won't be long before we die—we won't be here much longer!—so even if anyone offers us incredible wealth, why should we want it? Who could really own it? Who could really control it?

If you can read yourself in this matter, you come to a feeling of dispassion. Disenchantment. You lose your taste for all the lures of the world. You no longer hold them in esteem. If you make use of them, it's for the sake of the benefits they give in terms of the Dhamma, but your disenchantment stays continuous. Even the name and form you've been regarding as "me" and "mine" have been wearing down and falling apart continually. As for the defilements, they're still lying in wait to burn you. So how can you afford to be oblivious? First there's the suffering and stress of the five aggregates, and on top of that there's the suffering and stress caused by defilement, craving, and attachment, stabbing you, slapping you, beating you.

The more you practice and contemplate, the more you become deeply sensitive to this. Your interest in blatant things outside— good and bad people, good and bad things—gets swept away. You don't have to concern yourself with them, for you're concerned solely with penetrating yourself within, destroying your pride and conceit. Outside affairs aren't important. What's important is how clearly you can see the truth inside until the brightness appears.

The brightness that comes from seeing the truth isn't at all like the light we see outside. Once you really know it, you see that it's indescribable, for it's something entirely personal. It cleans everything out of the heart and mind in line with the strength of our mindfulness and discernment. It's what sweeps and cleans and clears and lets go and disbands things inside. But if we don't have mindfulness and discernment as our means of knowing, contemplating, and letting go, then everything inside is dark on all sides. And not only dark, but also full of fire whose poisonous fuel keeps burning away. What could be more terrifying than the fuel burning inside us? Even though it's invisible, it flares up every time there's sensory contact.

The bombs they drop on people to wipe them out aren't really all that dangerous, for you can die only once per lifetime. But the three bombs of passion, aversion, and delusion keep exploding the heart and mind countless times. Normally we don't realize how serious the damage is, but when we come to practice the Dhamma we can take stock of the situation, seeing what it's like when sensory contact comes, at what moments the burning heat of defilement and craving arises, and why they're all so very quick.

If you contemplate how to disband suffering and defilement, you need the proper tools and have to make the effort without being complacent. The fact that we've come to practice here, leaving behind our involvements or worldly responsibilities, helps speed up the practice. It's extremely beneficial in helping us to examine our inner diseases in detail and to disband suffering and stress continually. Our burdens grow lighter and we come to realize how much our practice of the Dhamma is progressing in the direction of the cessation of suffering.

Those who don't have the time to come and rest here, let alone to really stop, get carried away with all kinds of distractions. They may say, "I can practice anywhere," but it's just words. The fact of the matter is that their practice is to follow the defilements until their heads are spinning, and yet they can still boast that they can practice anywhere! Their mouths aren't in line with their minds, and their minds—burned and beaten by defilement, craving, and attachment—don't realize their situation. They're like worms that live in filth and are happy to stay and die right there in the filth.

People with any mindfulness and discernment feel disgust at the filth of the defilements in the mind. The more they practice, the more sensitive they become, the more their revulsion grows. Before, when our mindfulness and discernment were still crude, we didn't feel this. We were happy to play around in the filth within ourselves. But now that we've come to practice, to contemplate from the blatant to the more subtle levels, we sense more and more how disgusting the filth really is. There's nothing to it that's worth falling for, because it's all inconstancy, stress, and not-self.

So what's there to want out of life? Those who are ignorant say that we're born to gain wealth and be millionaires, but that kind of life is like falling into hell! If you understand the practice of the Dhamma in the Buddha's footsteps, you realize that nothing is worth having, nothing is worth getting involved with, everything has to be let go.

Those who still latch onto the body, feeling, perceptions, thought-fabrications, and consciousness as self need to contemplate until they see that the body is stressful, feelings are stressful, perceptions are stressful, thought-fabrications are stressful, consciousness is stressful—in short, name is stressful and so is form, or in even plainer terms, the body is stressful and so is the mind. *You have to focus on stress.* Once you see it thoroughly, from the blatant levels to the subtle, you'll be able to rise above pleasure and pain because you've let them go. But if you have yet to fully understand stress, you'll still yearn for pleasure—and the more you yearn, the more you suffer.

This holds too for the pleasure that comes when the mind is tranquil. If you let yourself get stuck on it, you're like a person addicted to a drug: Once there's the desire, you take the drug and consider yourself happy. But as for the suffering the repeated desire causes, you don't have the intelligence to see it. All you see is that if you take the drug whenever you want, you're okay.

When people can't shake off their addictions, this is why. They get stuck on the pleasure of taking the drug. They're ingesting sensuality and they keep on wanting more, for only when they ingest more will their hunger subside. But soon the hunger comes back again, so they want still more. They keep on ingesting sensuality, stirring up the mind, but don't see that there's any harm or suffering involved. Instead, they say they're happy. When the longing gets really intense, it feels really good to satisfy it. That's what they say. People who have heavy defilements and crude discernment don't see that desire and longing are suffering, and so they don't know how to do away with them. As soon as they take what they want, the desire goes away. Then it comes back again, so they take some more. It comes back again and they take still more, over and over, so blind that they don't realize anything at all.

People of intelligence, though, contemplate: "Why is there desire and why do I have to satisfy it? And when it comes back, why do I have to keep satisfying it over and over again?" *Once they realize that the desire itself is what they have to attack,* that by disbanding this one thing they won't feel any disturbance and will never have to suffer from desire again, *that's when they really can gain release from suffering and stress.* But for the most part we don't see things from this angle because we still find pleasure in consuming things. This is why it's hard for us to practice to abandon desire. All we know is how to feed on the bait, so we don't dare try giving it up—as when people who are addicted to eating meat are afraid to become vegetarians. Why? Because they're still attached to flavor, still slaves to desire.

If you can't let go of these blatant things, can you hope to abandon the damp, fermenting desires within you, so much harder to detect? You still take the most blatant baits. When desire whispers and pleads with you, there you go—pandering to it immediately. You don't notice how desire tires you out, how it's the source of the most vicious sufferings. Even though the Buddha teaches us to use our discernment to contemplate cause and effect in this area, we don't make the effort and instead keep swallowing the bait. We get our pleasure and that's all we want, going with the flow of craving and defilement.

Our practice here is to go *against* the flow of desire and mental wandering. It means self-restraint and training in many, many areas. For instance, when a sight, sound, smell, taste, or tactile sensation arises, we deceive ourselves into liking it and then, a moment later, tire of it and want something else. We get so thoroughly deceived that we end up running frantically all over the place.

The virulent diseases in the mind are more than many. If you don't know how to deal with them, you'll remain under Māra's power. Those who have truly seen stress and suffering willingly put their lives on the line in their effort to work free, in the same way the Buddha willingly put his life on the line in order to gain freedom from suffering and release from the world. He wasn't out after personal comfort. Each Buddha-to-be has had to undergo suffering in the world for his own sake and that of others. Each has had to relinquish all of his vast wealth instead of using it for his comfort. So the practice is one of struggle and endurance. Whoever struggles and endures will gain victory—and no other victory can match it. *Gaining control over the defilements is the ultimate victory.* Whatever you contemplate, you can let go—that's the ultimate victory.

So please keep up the effort. Don't let yourself relax after each little victory. The more victorious you are, the stronger, more daring, and more resilient your mindfulness and discernment will become, examining everything regardless of whether it comes by way of the eyes, ears, nose, tongue, body, or mind.

The more you examine yourself, the sharper your mindfulness and discernment will become. As soon as there's attachment, you'll see the suffering and stress—just as when you touch fire, feel the heat, and immediately let go. This is why the practice of the Dhamma is of supreme worth. It's not a game you play—for the defilements have a great deal of power that's hard to overcome. But if you make the effort to overcome them, they'll weaken as mindfulness and discernment grow stronger. This is when you can say that you're making progress in the Dhamma: when you can disband your own suffering and stress.

So try to go all the way while you still have the breath to breathe. The Buddha said, "Make an effort to attain the as-yet-unattained, reach the as-yet-unreached, realize the as-yet-unrealized." He didn't want us to be weak and vacillating, always making excuses for ourselves, because now that we're ordained we've already made an important sacrifice. In the Buddha's time, no matter where the monks and nuns came from—from royal, wealthy, or ordinary backgrounds—once they had left their homes they cut their family ties and entered the Lord Buddha's lineage without ever returning. To return to the home life, he said, was to become a person of no worth. His only concern was to keep pulling people out, pulling them out of suffering and stress. If we want to escape, we have to follow his example, cutting away worry and concern for our family and relatives by entering his lineage. To live and practice under his discipline is truly the supreme refuge, the supreme way.

Those who follow the principles of the Dhamma-Vinaya—even though they may have managed only an occasional taste of its peace without yet reaching the paths and their fruitions—pledge their lives to the Buddha, Dhamma, and Sangha. They realize that nothing else they can reach will lead to freedom from suffering, but if they reach this one refuge, they'll gain total release. Those whose mindfulness and discernment are deep, far-seeing, and meticulous will cross over to the far shore. They've lived long enough on this shore and have had all the suffering they can bear. They've circled around in birth and death countless times. Realizing now that they must reach the far shore, they make a relentless effort to let go of their sense of self.

There's nothing distant about the far shore, but to get there you have to give up your sense of self by investigating the five aggregates and seeing them all as stress, not "me" or "mine." Focus on the single theme of not clinging. The Lord Buddha once spoke of the past as below, the future as above, and the present as in the middle. He also said that unskillful qualities are below, skillful qualities above, and neutral ones in the middle. Of each of them, he said, "Don't cling to it." Even *nibbāna,* the far shore, shouldn't be clung to. *See how far we're going to be released through not clinging!* Any of you who can't comprehend that even *nibbāna* isn't to be clung to should consider the standard teaching that tells us not to cling, that we have to let go: "All things are unworthy of attachment." This is the ultimate summary of all that the Buddha taught.

All phenomena, whether compounded or uncompounded, fall under the phrase *"sabbe dhammā anattā*—all phenomena are not-self." They're all unworthy of attachment. This summarizes everything, including our investigation to see the truth of the world and of the Dhamma, to see things clearly with our mindfulness and discernment, penetrating through the compounded to the uncompounded, or through the worldly to the transcendent, all of which has to be done by looking within, not without.

And if we want to see the real essence of the Dhamma, we have to look deeply, profoundly. Then it's simply a matter of letting go all along the way. We see all the way in and let go of everything. The theme of *not clinging* covers everything from beginning to end. If our practice is correct, it's because we penetrate everything with mindfulness and discernment, not getting stuck on any form, feeling, perception, thought-fabrication, or consciousness at all.

The Buddha taught about how ignorance—not knowing form, being deluded about form—leads to craving, the mental act that arises at the mind and agitates it, leading to the *kamma* by which we try to get what we crave. When you understand this, you can practice correctly, for you know that you have to disband the craving. The reason we contemplate the body and mind over and over is so that we won't feel desire for anything outside, won't get engrossed in anything outside. The more you contemplate, the more things outside seem pitiful and not worth getting engrossed in. The reason you were engrossed and excited was because you didn't know. And so you raved about people and things and made a lot of fuss, talking about worldly matters: "This is good, that's bad, she's good, he's bad." The mind got all scattered in worldly affairs—and so how could you examine the diseases within your own mind?

The Buddha answered Mogharāja's question—In what way does one view the world so as not to be seen by the King of Death?—by telling him to view the world as empty of self. We have to strip away conventions such as "person" and "being," and all designations such as properties, aggregates, and sense media. Once we know how to strip away conventions and designations, there's nothing we need to hold on to. What's left is the deathless, the transcendent, *nibbāna*. There are many names for it, but they're all one and the same. When you strip away all worldly things, what's left is the transcendent. When you strip away all compounded things, what's left is the uncompounded, the true Dhamma.

So consider whether this is worth attaining. If we stay in the world, we have to go through repeated births and deaths in the three levels of existence: sensuality, form, and formlessness. But on that far shore there's no birth, no death. It's beyond the reach of the King of Death. But because we don't know the far shore, we want to keep on being reborn on this shore with its innumerable repeated sufferings.

Once you comprehend suffering and stress, though, there's nowhere else you want to turn: You head straight for the far shore, the shore with no birth or death, the shore where defilement and craving disband once and for all. Your practice thus goes straight to the cessation of suffering and defilement, to clear penetration of the common characteristics of inconstancy, stress, and not-selfness in the aggregates. People with mindfulness and discernment focus their contemplation in the direction of absolute disbanding, for if their disbanding isn't absolute, they'll have to be reborn again in suffering and stress. So keep disbanding attachments, keep letting go, keep contemplating inconstancy, stress, and not-selfness, and keep relinquishing them. This is the right path for sure.

Isn't this something worth knowing and training for? It's not all that mysterious or faraway, you know. It's something that any-one—man or woman—can realize, something we can all train in. We can develop virtue, make the mind quiet, and use our mindfulness and discernment to contemplate. So isn't this really worth practicing?

Stupid people say no. They say they can't do it: can't observe the precepts, can't make the mind quiet. It's the best thing in life—

the practice for release from suffering and stress—and yet they reject it. Instead they rush around in a turmoil, competing with one another and bragging about themselves, and then end up rotting in their coffins. Exactly what is appealing about all that?

We've gone astray for far too long already, our lives almost gone after how many decades. Now we've come here to turn ourselves around. No matter how old you are, the air you breathe isn't just for your convenience and comfort, but for you to learn about stress. That way you'll be able to disband it. Don't imagine that your family and relatives are essential to you. You are alone. You came alone and you'll go alone. *Only when there's no "you," no self, to go:* That's when you penetrate to the Dhamma. If there's still a self to be born, then you're stuck in the cycle of suffering and stress. So isn't it worthwhile to strive for release? It's something only you can find for yourself.

Those who trust in the Lord Buddha will all have to follow this path. To trust the defilements is to get stuck fast in a mire—and when you're there, who will you be able to brag to, aside from your own sufferings? The knowledge that leads to dispassion and disenchantment is what counts as true knowledge. But if your knowledge leads you to hold on, then you're a disciple of Māra. You still find things very delicious. You may say that you're disenchanted, but the mind isn't disenchanted at all. It still wants to take this, to get that, to stay right here.

Whoever can keep reading the truth within the mind, deeper and deeper, will get all the way through, having wiped out stupidity and delusion at each step along the way. You used to be deluded; now you come to your senses. You used to brag; now you realize how very stupid you were—and you understand that you'll have to keep on correcting your stupidity.

Reading yourself, contemplating yourself, you see new angles, you gain more precise self-knowledge each step along the way. It's not a question of being an expert about things outside. You see how what's inside is really inconstant, really stressful, really not-self. You used to fall for things and latch onto them because of your blindness, because you didn't understand. Who can you blame for that? Your own stupidity, that's who—because it wanted to brag about how much it knew.

Now you know that you've still got a lot of stupidity left and that you'll have to get rid of it before you die. Every day that you still have breath left to breathe, use it to wipe out your stupidity rather than to get this or be that or to dance around. The ones who dance around are possessed by spirits. The demons of defilement make them crazy and delude them into wanting to get this and be that and dance all over the place. But if you focus your attention on yourself, then your pride, your conceit, your desires to stand out will shrink out of sight, never daring to show their faces for the rest of your life, for you realize that the more you brag, the more you suffer.

So the essence of the practice is to turn around and focus inside. The more you can wash away these things, the more empty and free the mind will be: This is its own reward. If you connive with your conceit, you'll destroy whatever virtue you have, but if you can drive these demons away, virtuous ones will come and stay with you. If the demons are still there, the virtuous ones won't be able to stay. They can't get along at all. If you let yourself get entangled in turmoil, it's an affair of the demons. If you're empty and free, it's an affair of cleanliness and peace—an affair of the virtuous ones.

So go and check how many of these demons you've been able to sweep away. Are they thinning out? When they make an appearance, point at them right in the face and call them what they are: demons and devils, here to eat your heart and drink your blood. You've let them eat you before, but now you've finally come to your senses and can drive them away. That will put an end to your troubles, or at least lighten your suffering. Your sense of self will start to shrivel away. Before, it was big, fat, and powerful, but now its power is gone. Your pride and conceit have grown thin and weak. It's as when a person has been bitten by a rabid dog: They give him a serum made from rabid dogs to drive out the disease. The same holds here. If we can recognize these things, they disband. The mind is then empty and at peace, for this one thing—the theme of not clinging—can disband suffering and stress with every moment.

SIMPLY STOP RIGHT HERE

The way we've been contemplating makes us realize how giving rise to genuine mindfulness and discernment is a process of disbanding suffering and defilement. Whenever mindfulness lapses and we latch onto something, our practice of reading ourselves step by step will enable us to realize the situation easily. This helps us keep the mind under control and does a world of good. Still, it's not enough, for the affairs of suffering and defilement are paramount issues buried deep in the character. Thus we have to contemplate and examine things within ourselves.

Looking outside is something we're used to. Whenever we know things outside, the mind is in a turmoil instead of being empty and at peace. We can all be aware of this. And this is why we have to maintain the mind in its state of neutrality or mindful centeredness. We then examine our experience in the practice: What state have we been able to maintain the mind in? Is our mindfulness continuous throughout all our activities? We have to observe these things. When the mind deviates from its foundation because of mental fabrications, habitually creating all sorts of turmoil, what can we do to make it settle down and grow still? If it doesn't grow still, it gets involved in nothing but stress: wandering around thinking, imagining, taking on all sorts of things. *That's* stress. You have to keep reading these things at all times, seeing clearly the ways in which they're inconstant, changing, and stressful.

Now if you watch the arising and passing away within yourself, you understand that it is neither good nor bad. It's simply a natural process of arising, persisting, and passing away. Try to see deeply into this. When you do, you'll be sweeping the mind clean, just as when you constantly sweep out your house: If anything then comes to make it dirty, you'll be able to detect it. So with every moment, we have to sweep out whatever arises, persists, and then passes away. Let it all pass away, without latching on or clinging to anything. Try to make the mind aware of this state of nonattachment within itself. If the mind doesn't latch onto anything, doesn't cling to anything, there's no commotion in it. It's empty and at peace.

This state of awareness is *so* worth knowing, for it doesn't require that you know a lot of other things at all. You simply have to contemplate the inconstancy of form, feelings, perceptions, thought-fabrications, and consciousness. Or you can contemplate whatever preoccupies the mind as it continually changes—arising and passing away—with every moment. This is something you have to contemplate until you really *know* it. Otherwise, you'll fall for your preoccupations in line with the way you label sensory contacts. If you don't fall for sensory contacts arising in the present, you fall for your memories or thought-fabrications. This is why you have to train the mind to stay firmly centered in neutrality without latching onto anything at all. *If you can maintain this one stance continuously, you'll be sweeping everything out of the mind,* disbanding its suffering and stress in the immediate present with each and every moment.

Everything arises and then passes away, arises and then passes away—everything. Don't grasp hold of anything, thinking that it's good or bad or taking it as your self. Stop all your discursive thinking and mental fabrications. When you can maintain this state of awareness, the mind will calm down on its own, will naturally become empty and free. If any thoughts arise, see that they just come and go, and don't latch onto them. When you can read the aspects of the mind that arise and pass away, there's not much else to do. Just keep watching and letting go, and you'll have no lasting, drawn-out trains of thought about the past or future. They all stop right at the arising and passing away.

When you really see the present with its arisings and passings away, there are no great issues. Whatever you think about will all pass away, *but if you can't notice its passing away, you'll grasp at whatever comes up,* and then everything will become a turmoil of ceaseless imaginings. So you have to cut off these connected thought-fabrications that keep flowing like a stream. Establish your mindfulness and, once it's established, simply fix your whole attention on the mind. Then you'll be able to still the flow of thought-fabrications that distracted you. Do this at any time, and the mind will become still and empty, unentangled, unattached. Then keep watch over the normalcy of the mind again and again whenever it gets engrossed and starts spinning out long, drawn-out thought-fabrications. As soon as you're aware, let them stop. If you let them stop right then, things will disband. Whatever the issue, disband it immediately. Practice like this until you become skilled at it, and the mind won't get involved in distractions.

It's like driving a car: When you want to stop, just slam on the brakes and you stop immediately. The same principle works with the mind. You'll notice that, no matter when, as soon as there's mindfulness, it stops and grows still. In other words, when mindfulness is firmly centered, then no matter what happens, as soon as you're mindfully aware of it, the mind stops, disengages, and is free. This is a simple method: stopping as soon as you're mindful. Any other approach is just too slow to cope. This method of examining yourself, knowing yourself, is very worth knowing because anyone can apply it at any time. Even right here while I'm speaking and you're listening, just focus your attention right at the mind as it's normal in the present. This is an excellent way of knowing your own mind.

Before we knew anything about all this, we let the mind go chasing after any thoughts that occurred to it, taking up a new thought as soon as it was finished with an old one, spinning its webs to trap us in all kinds of complications. Whatever meditation techniques we tried weren't really able to stop our distraction. So don't underestimate this method as being too simple. Train yourself to be on top of any objects that make contact or any opinions that intrude on your awareness. When pride and opinions come pouring out, cry, "Stop! Let me first have *my* say!" This method of calling a halt can really still the defilements immediately, even when they're like two people interrupting each other to speak, the conceit or sense of "self" on one side immediately raising objections before the other side has even finished. Or you might say it's like suddenly running into a dangerous beast—a tiger or poisonous snake—with no means of escape. All you can do is simply stop, totally still, and spread thoughts of loving-kindness.

The same holds true here. You simply stop, and that cuts the strength of the defilement or any sense of self that's made a sudden appearance. We have to stop the defilements in their tracks, for if we don't, they'll grow strong and keep intensifying. So we have to stop them right from the first. Resist them right from the first. This way your mindfulness will get used to dealing with them. As soon as you say, "Stop!" things stop immediately. The defilements will grow obedient and won't dare push you around in any way.

If you're going to sit for an hour, make sure that you're mindful right at the mind the whole time. Don't just aim at the pleasure of tranquillity. Sit and watch the sensations within the mind to see how it's centered. Don't concern yourself with any cravings or feelings that arise. Even if pain arises, in whatever way, don't pay it any attention. Keep being mindful of the centered normalcy of the mind at all times. The mind won't stray off to any pleasures or pains but will let go of them all, seeing the pains as an affair of the aggregates, because the aggregates are inconstant. Feelings are inconstant. The body's inconstant. That's the way they have to be.

When a pleasant feeling arises, the craving for pleasure wants to stay with that feeling as long as possible. But when there's pain, it acts in an entirely opposite way, because pain hurts. When pains arise as we sit for long periods of time, the mind gets agitated because craving pushes for a change. It wants us to adjust things in this way or that. *We have to train ourselves to disband the craving instead.* If pains grow strong in the body, we have to practice staying at equanimity by realizing that they're the pains of the aggregates—and not our pain—until the mind is no longer agitated and can return to a normal state of equanimity.

Even if the equanimity isn't complete, don't worry about it. Simply make sure that the mind doesn't struggle to change the situation. Keep disbanding the struggling, the craving. If the pain is so unbearable that you have to change positions, don't make the change while the mind is really worked up. Keep sitting still, watch how far the pain goes, and change positions only when the right moment comes. Then as you stretch out your leg, make sure that the mind is still centered, still at equanimity. Stay that way for about five minutes, and the fierce pain will go away. But watch out. When a pleasant feeling replaces the pain, the mind will like it. So use mindfulness to keep the mind neutral and at equanimity.

Practice this in all your activities, because the mind tends to get engrossed with pleasant feelings. It can even get engrossed with neutral feelings. So you have to keep your mindfulness firmly established, knowing feelings for what they really are: inconstant and stressful, with no real pleasure to them at all. Contemplate pleasant feelings to see them as nothing but stress. You have to keep doing this at all times. Don't get infatuated with pleasant feelings, for if you do, you fall into more suffering and stress because craving wants nothing but pleasure even though the aggregates have no pleasure to offer. The physical and mental aggregates are all stressful. If the mind can rise above pleasure, above pain, above feeling, *right there is where it gains release.* Please understand this. It's released from feeling. If the mind hasn't yet gained release from feeling, if it still wants pleasure, if it's still attached to pleasure and pain, then try to notice the state of mind at the moments when it's neutral toward feeling. That will enable it to gain release from suffering and stress.

So we have to practice a lot with feelings of physical pain and, at the same time, we have to try to comprehend pleasant feelings as well, for the pleasant feelings connected with the subtle defilements of passion and craving are things we don't really understand. We think that they're true pleasure, which makes us want them. This wanting is craving—and the Buddha tells us to abandon craving and passion for name and form. "Passion" here means wanting to get nothing but pleasure and then becoming entangled in liking or disliking what results. It means that we're entangled in the delicious flavors of feelings, regardless of whether they're physical feelings or mental ones.

We should realize that when a feeling of physical pain gets very strong, we *can* handle it by using mindfulness to keep the mind from struggling. Then, even if there's a great deal of physical pain, we can let go. Even though the body may be agitated, the mind isn't agitated along with it. But to do this, you first have to practice separating feelings from the mind while you're still strong and healthy.

As for the feelings that come with desire, if we accumulate them, they lead to even greater suffering. Don't think of them as being easeful or comfortable, because that's delusion. You have to keep track of how feelings—no matter which sort they are—are all inconstant, stressful, and not-self. If you can let go of feeling, you'll become disenchanted with form, feelings, perceptions, thought-fabrications, and consciousness that carry feelings of pleasure. But if you don't contemplate these things, you'll stay infatuated.

So try noticing when the mind is in this infatuated state. Is it empty and at peace? If it's attached, you'll see that it's dirty and defiled because it's deluded into clinging. As soon as there's pain, it grows all agitated. If the mind is addicted to the three kinds of feeling—pleasant, painful, and neither pleasant nor painful—it has to endure suffering and stress. We have to see the inconstancy, stressfulness, and not-selfness of the body and mind so that we won't cling. We won't cling whether we look outside or in. We'll be empty—empty because of our lack of attachment. We'll know that the mind isn't suffering from stress. The more deeply we look inside, the more we'll see that the mind is empty of attachment.

This is how we gain release from suffering and stress. It's the simplest way to gain release, but if we don't really understand, it's the hardest. Thus it's extremely essential that you practice letting go. The moment the mind latches onto anything, you can really make it let go. And then notice that when you tell the mind to let go, it lets go. When you tell it to stop, it stops. When you tell it to be empty, it's really empty.

This method of watching the mind is extremely useful, but we're rarely interested in becoming skillful and resourceful at disbanding our own sufferings. We practice in a leisurely, casual way and don't know which points we should correct, where we should disband things, what we should let go of. And so we keep circling around with suffering and attachment.

We have to find an opportunity to disband suffering with every moment. We can't just live, sleep, and eat at our ease. We need to find ways to examine and contemplate all things, using our mindfulness and discernment to see their emptiness of "self." Only then will we be able to loosen our attachments. If we don't know with real mindfulness and discernment, our practice won't be able to lead us out of suffering and stress.

Every defilement—each one in the classical list of sixteen (see Glossary)—is hard to abandon Still, they don't arise all sixteen at once, but only one at a time. If you know the features of their arising, you can let them go. The first step is to recognize their faces clearly, because you have to realize that they're burning hot every time they arise. If they have you sad or upset, it's easy to know them. If they have you happy, they're harder to detect. So you first have to learn to recognize the mind at normalcy, keeping your words and deeds at normalcy, too. "Normalcy" here means being free of liking and disliking. It's a question of purity in virtue—just as when we practice restraint of the senses. Normalcy is the basic foundation. If the mind isn't at normalcy—if it likes this or dislikes that—that means that your restraint of the senses isn't pure. For instance, when you see a sight with the eye or hear a sound with the ear, you don't get upset as long as no real pains arise, but if you get distracted and absentminded as the pains get more and more intense, your precepts will suffer, and you'll end up all agitated.

So don't underestimate even the smallest things. Use your mindfulness and discernment to disband things, to destroy them, and to keep working at your investigation. Then, even if serious events happen, you'll be able to let go of them. If your attachments are heavy, you'll be able to let go of them. If they're many, you'll be able to thin them out.

The same holds true with intermediate defilements: the Five Hindrances. Any liking for sights, sounds, smells, tastes, and tactile sensations is the hindrance of sensual desire. If you don't like what you see, hear, etc., that's the hindrance of ill will. These hindrances of liking and disliking defile the mind, making it agitated and scattered, unable to grow calm. Try observing the mind when it's dominated by the Five Hindrances to see whether or not it's in a state of suffering. Do you recognize these intermediate defilements when they enshroud your mind?

The hindrance of sensual desire is like a dye that clouds clear water, making it murky—and when the mind is murky, it's suffering. The hindrance of ill will is irritability and dissatisfaction, and the hindrance of sloth and torpor is a state of drowsiness and lethargy—a condition of refusing to deal with anything at all, burying yourself in sleep and lazy forgetfulness. All the hindrances, including the final pair—restlessness/anxiety and uncertainty—cloak the mind in darkness. This is why you need to be resilient in fighting them off and in investigating them, so that you can weaken and eliminate them all, from the gross to the middling and on to the subtle.

The practice of the Dhamma is very delicate work, requiring that you use all your mindfulness and discernment in probing and comprehending the body and mind. When you look into the body, try to see the truth of how it's inconstant, stressful, and nothing more than physical elements. If you don't contemplate in this way, your practice will simply grope around and won't be able to release you from suffering and stress—for the sufferings caused by the defilements concocting things in the mind are more than many. The mind is full of all kinds of tricks. Sometimes you may gain some insight through mindfulness and discernment—becoming bright, empty, and at peace—only to find the defilements slipping in to spoil things, cloaking the mind in total darkness once more.

We each have to find special strategies in reading ourselves so that we don't get lost in distractions. Desire is a big troublemaker here, and so is distraction. Torpor and lethargy—*all* the hindrances—are enemies blocking your way. The fact that you haven't seen anything all the way through is because these characters are blocking your way and have you surrounded. You have to find a way to destroy them using *apt attention*—in other words, a skillful way of making use of the mind. You have to dig down and explore, contemplating how these things arise, how they pass away, and what exactly is inconstant, stressful, and not-self. These are questions you have to keep asking yourself so that the mind will really come to know. When you really know inconstancy, you're sure to let go of defilement, craving, and attachment, or at least be able to weaken and thin them out. It's like having a broom in your hand. Whenever attachment arises, you sweep it away until the mind can no longer grow attached to anything, for there's nothing left for it to be attached to. You've seen that everything is inconstant, so what's there to latch onto?

When you're persistent in contemplating your inconstancy, stress, and not-selfness, the mind feels at ease because you've loosened your attachments. This is the marvel of the Dhamma: an ease of body and mind completely free from entanglement in the defilements. It's truly special. Before, the ignorance obscuring the mind caused you to wander about, spellbound by sights, sounds, and so forth. Defilement, craving, and attachment had you under their power. But now, mindfulness and discernment break the spell by seeing that there's no self to these things, nothing real to them at all. They simply arise and pass away with every moment. There's not the least little bit of "me" or "mine" to them. Once we really know with mindfulness and discernment, we sweep everything clean, leaving nothing but pure Dhamma with no sense of self at all. We see nothing but inconstancy, stress, and not-selfness, with no pleasure or pain.

The Lord Buddha taught, *"Sabbe dhammā anattā—*All phenomena are not-self." Both the fabricated and the unfabricated— which is *nibbāna,* the transcendent—are not-self. There's just Dhamma. *This is very important.* There's no sense of self there, but what *is* there, is Dhamma. This isn't the extinction taught by the wrong view of annihilationism; it's the extinction of all attachment to "me" and "mine." All that remains is deathlessness—the undying Dhamma, the undying property—free from birth, aging, illness, and death. Everything still remains as it was, it hasn't been annihilated anywhere; the only things annihilated are the defilements together with all suffering and stress. It's called *suñño*—empty— because it's empty of the label of self. *This deathlessness is the true marvel the Buddha discovered and taught to awaken us.*

This is why it's worth penetrating clear through the inconstancy, stress, and not-selfness of the five aggregates, for what then remains is the natural Dhamma free from birth, aging, illness, and death. It's called Unbinding, Emptiness, the Unfabricated: These names all mean the same thing. They're simply conventional designations that you must learn to let go so that you can dwell in the aspect of mind devoid of any sense of self.

So the paths, fruitions, and *nibbāna* are not something to hope for in a future life by developing a vast heap of perfections. Some people like to point out that the Lord Buddha had to accumulate so many virtues—but what about you? Consider how many lives have passed without your attaining the goal, all because of your stupidity in continually finding excuses for yourself.

The basic principles that the Lord Buddha taught—such as the four establishings of mindfulness, the four Noble Truths, the three characteristics of inconstancy, stress, and not-selfness—are right here inside you, so probe and contemplate them until you know them. Defilement, craving, and attachment are right here inside you, too, so contemplate them until you gain true insight. Then you'll be able to let them go, no longer latching onto them as really being "me" or "mine." This way you'll gain release from suffering and stress within yourself.

Don't keep excusing yourself by relying, for instance, on the miraculous powers of some object or by waiting to build up the perfections. Don't think in those terms. Think instead of what the defilements are like right here and now: Is it better to disband them or to fall in with them? If you fall in with them, is there suffering and stress? You have to find out the truth within yourself so as to get rid of your stupidity and delusion in thinking that this bodily frame of suffering is really happiness.

We're all stuck in this delusion because we don't open our eyes. This is why we have to keep discussing these issues, giving advice, and digging out the truth so that you'll give rise to the mindfulness and discernment that will enable you to know yourself. It's good that you've begun to see things, to acknowledge the defilements and stress within yourself at least to some extent. It's better that we talk about these things, about how to contemplate body, feelings, mind, and mental qualities so as to disband our suffering and stress. This way we can reduce our sufferings by letting go of the defilements that agitate and scorch the mind. Our mindfulness and discernment will gradually be able to eliminate the defilements and cravings from the heart.

This practice of ours, if we really work at it, will greatly reduce our suffering. This will attract others to follow our example. We won't have to advertise, for they'll have to notice. We don't have to brag about what level we've attained or what degrees we've earned. We don't have any of that here, for all we talk about is suffering, stress, the defilements, not-self. If we know with real mindfulness and discernment, we can scrape away our defilements, cravings, and attachments, and the good results will be right there inside us.

So now that we have this opportunity, we should make a concerted effort to make progress. Don't let your life pass by under the influence of defilement, craving, and attachment. Make an effort to correct yourself in this area every day, every moment, and you're sure to progress in your practice of destroying your defilements and disbanding your suffering and stress. This business of sacrificing defilements or sacrificing your sense of self is very important because it gives rewards—peace, normalcy, freedom with every moment— *right here in the heart.* The practice is thus something really worthy of interest. If you're not interested in the practice of searching out and destroying the diseases of defilement, of your own suffering and stress, you'll stay stuck in repeated suffering like all ignorant persons.

When Māra—temptation—tried to stop the Buddha's efforts by telling him that within seven days he would become a Universal Emperor, the Buddha answered, "I know already! Don't try to deceive me or tempt me." Because the Buddha had the ability to know such things instantly for himself, Māra was continually defeated. But what about you? Are you a disciple of the Lord Buddha or of Māra? Whenever temptation appears—there you go, following Māra hook, line, and sinker with no sense of weariness or dispassion at all. If we're really disciples of the Buddha we have to go *against* the flow of defilement, craving, and attachment, establishing ourselves in good qualities—beginning with morality, which forms the ideal principle for protecting ourselves. Then we can gain release from suffering by working from the level of the precepts, developing mental calm, and then using discernment to see inconstancy, stress, and not-self. This is a high level of discernment, you know: the discernment that penetrates not-self.

At any rate, the important point is not to believe your defilements. Even though you may still have the fermentations of ignorance or craving in your mind, always keep making use of mindfulness and discernment as your means of knowing, letting go, scrubbing things clean. When these fermentations come to tempt you, simply stop. Let go. Refuse to go along with them. If you believe them when they tell you to latch onto things, you'll get agitated and burn with desire. But if you don't go along with them, the desires will gradually loosen, subside, and eventually cease.

So in training the mind, you have to take desire as your battlefield in the same way you would in treating an addiction: If you aren't intent on defeating it, there's no way you can escape being a slave to it repeatedly. You have to use mindfulness as a protective shield and discernment as your weapon to cut through and destroy your desires. If you do so, your practice will steadily progress, enabling you to keep abreast of defilement, craving, and attachment with ever more precision.

If, in your practice, you can read and decipher the mind, you'll find your escape route, following the footsteps of the Noble Ones. But as long as you don't see it, you'll think that there are no paths, no fruitions, no *nibbāna*. *Only when you can disband the defilements will you know.* You really have to be able to disband them in order to know for yourself that the paths, fruitions, and *nibbāna* really exist and really can disband suffering and stress. They're timeless. No matter what the time or season, whenever you have the mindfulness to stop and let go, there's no suffering. As you learn to do this over and over, more and more frequently, the defilements grow weaker and weaker. This is why it's *ehipassiko*—something you can invite other people to "come and see"—for all people who do this can disband defilement and suffering. If they contemplate until they see inconstancy, stress, and not-self, they'll no longer have any attachments, and their minds will become Dhamma, will become free.

There's no need to get all excited about anyone outside—spirit entities or whatever—because success in the practice lies right here in the heart. Look into it until you penetrate clearly all the way through yourself, sweep away all your attachments, and then you'll have this *ehipassiko* within you. "Come and see! Come and see!" But if there's still any defilement, then it's "Come and see! Come and see the defilements burning me!" It can work both ways, you know. If you disband the defilements, let go, and come to a stop, then it's "Come and see how the defilements are gone, how the mind is empty right here and now!" This is something anyone can know, something you can know thoroughly for yourself with no great difficulty.

Turning to look into the mind isn't all that difficult, you know. You don't have to travel far to do it. You can watch it at any time, in any posture. True things and false are all there within you, but if you don't study yourself within, you won't know them—for you spend all your time studying external matters, the things of the world that worldly people study. If you want to study the Dhamma, you have to turn around and come inside, watching right at the body, at feelings, at the mind, at mental qualities until you know the truth that the body isn't you or yours: It's inconstant, stressful, and not-self. Feelings are inconstant, stressful, and not-self. The mind is inconstant, stressful, and not-self as well. Then look at the Dhamma of mental qualities: They're inconstant and stressful. They arise, persist, and pass away. If you don't latch on and can become free from any sense of self right here in mental qualities, the mind becomes free.

If you understand correctly, the mind is really easy to deal with. If you don't, it's the exact opposite. It's like pushing a light switch. If you hit the On button, it's immediately bright. With the Off button, it's dark. The same holds true with the mind. If your knowledge is wrong, it's dark. If your knowledge is right, it's bright. Then look to see if there's anything worth clinging to. If you really look, you'll see that there isn't, for all the things you can cling to are suffering and stress—affairs of ignorance, speculation, daydreaming, taking issue with things, self, people, useless chatter, endless news reports. But if you focus on probing into the mind, there's nothing—nothing but letting go to be empty and free. This is where the Dhamma arises easily—as easily as defilements arise on the other side—simply because you're now looking from a different angle and have the choice: Do I want the dark or the bright? Should I stop or keep running? Should I be empty or entangled? It's up to you to decide.

The Dhamma is marvelous and amazing. If you start out with right understanding, you can understand it through and through. If you get snagged at any point, you can examine and contemplate things to see where you're still attached. Keep cross-examining back and forth, and then all will become clear.

We're already good at following the knowledge of defilement and craving, so now we have to follow the knowledge of mindfulness and discernment instead. Keep cross-examining the defilements. Don't submit to them easily. You have to resist their power and refuse to fall in with them. That's when you'll really come to understand. When you really understand, everything stops. Craving stops, your wanderings stop. Likes, hatreds—this knowledge sweeps everything away. But if you don't understand, you keep gathering things up until you're thoroughly embroiled, arranging this, adjusting that, wanting this, rejecting that, letting your sense of self rear its ugly head.

Think of it like this: You're a huge playhouse showing a true-to-life drama whose hero, heroine, and villains—which are conventional suppositions—are entirely within you. If you strip away all conventional suppositions and designations, what you have left is nothing but Dhamma: freedom, emptiness. And simply being free and empty of any sense of self is enough to bring the whole show to an end.

A GOOD DOSE OF DHAMMA: FOR MEDITATORS WHEN THEY ARE ILL

Normally, illness is something we all have, but the type of illness where you can still do your work isn't recognized as illness. It's called the normal human condition all over the world. Yet really, when the body is in its normal state, it's still ill. But people generally are unaware of this illness: the deterioration of physical and mental phenomena, continually, from moment to moment.

The way people get carried away with their thoughts and preoccupations while they're still strong enough to work—that's real complacency. They're no match for people lying in bed ill. People lying in bed ill are lucky because they have the opportunity to do nothing but contemplate stress and pain. Their minds don't take up anything else, don't go anywhere else. They can contemplate pain at all times—and let go of pain at all times, too.

Don't you see the difference? The "emptiness" of the mind when you're involved in activities is "play" emptiness, imitation emptiness. It's not the real thing. But to contemplate inconstancy, stress, and not-selfness as it appears right inside you while you're lying right here is very beneficial for you. Just don't think that *you're* what's hurting. Simply see the natural phenomena of physical and mental events as they arise and pass away, arise and pass away They're not you. They're not really yours. You don't have any real control over them.

Look at them! Exactly where do you have any control over them? This is true for everyone in the world. You're not the only one to whom it's happening. So whatever disease you have, it's not important. What's important is the disease in the mind. Normally we don't pay much attention to the fact that we have diseases in our minds—in other words, the diseases of defilement, craving, and attachment. We pay attention only to our physical diseases, afraid of all the horrible things that can happen to the body. But no matter how much we try to stave things off with our fears, when the time comes for things to happen, no matter what medicines you use to treat the body, you can win only temporary respite. Even the people in the past who *didn't* suffer from heavy diseases are no longer with us. They've all had to part from their bodies in the end.

When you continually contemplate like this, you see the truth of inconstancy, stress, and not-selfness correctly within you. And you grow more and more disenchanted with things, step by step.

When you give it a try and let go, who's there? Are *you* the one hurting, or is it simply an affair of the Dhamma? Examine carefully and you'll see that it's not really *you* that's hurting. *The disease isn't your disease. It's a disease of the body,* a disease of physical form. In the end, physical form and mental events are always changing, are stressful in the change, and are not-self in the change and stress. But you must focus on them, watch them, and contemplate them so that they're clear. Make this knowledge really clear, and right there is where you'll gain release from all suffering and stress. Right there is where you'll put an end to all suffering and stress. As for the aggregates, they'll continue to arise, age, grow ill, and pass away in line with their own affairs. When their causes and conditions run out, they die and go into their coffin.

Some people, when they're healthy and complacent, die suddenly and unexpectedly without knowing what's happening to them. Their minds are completely oblivious to what's going on. They are much worse off than the person lying ill in bed who has pain to contemplate and so can develop disenchantment. So you don't have to be afraid of pain. If it's going to be there, let it be there—but don't let the mind be in pain with it. And then ask yourself—right now: Is the mind empty of "me" and "mine"?

Keep on looking in. Keep on looking in so that things are really clear, and that's enough. You don't have to find out anything anywhere else. When you can cure the disease or the pain lightens, that's something normal. When it doesn't lighten, that's normal too. But if the heart is simply empty of "me" and "mine," there will be no pain within it. As for the pain in the aggregates, don't give it a second thought.

So see yourself as lucky. Lying here, dealing with the disease, you have the opportunity to practice insight meditation with every moment. It doesn't matter whether you're here in the hospital or at home. Don't let there be any real sense in the mind that you're in the hospital or at home. *Let the mind be in the emptiness,* empty of all labels and meanings. You don't have to label yourself as being anywhere at all.

This is because the aggregates are not where you are. They're empty of any indwelling person. They're empty of any "me" or "mine." When the mind is like this, it doesn't need anything at all.

It doesn't have to be here or go there or anywhere at all. This is the absolute end of suffering and stress.

The mind, when it's not engrossed with the taste of pleasure or pain, is free in line with its nature. But I ask that you watch it carefully, this mind when it's empty, when it's not concocting any desires for anything, not wanting pleasure or trying to push away pain.

When the mind is empty in line with its nature, there's no sense of ownership in it; there are no labels for itself. No matter what thoughts occur to it, it sees them as insubstantial, as empty of self. There's simply a sensation that then passes away. A sensation that passes away, and that's all.

So you have to watch the phenomena that arise and pass away. You have to watch the phenomenon of the present continuously— and the mind will be empty, in that it will give no meanings or labels to the arising and passing away. As for the arising and passing away, that's a characteristic of the aggregates in accordance with their normal nature—the empty mind simply isn't involved, doesn't latch on. This is the point you can make use of.

You can't prevent pleasure and pain, you can't keep the mind from labeling things and forming thoughts, *but you can put these things to a new use.* If the mind labels a pain, saying, "I hurt," you have to read the label carefully, contemplating it until you see that it's wrong. If the label were right, it would have to say that the pain isn't me, it's empty. Or if there's a thought that "I'm in pain," this type of thinking is also wrong. You have to take a new approach to your thinking, to see that thinking is inconstant, stressful, and not yours.

So whatever arises, investigate and let go of what's right in front of you. Just make sure that you don't cling, and the mind will keep on being empty in line with its nature. Maybe no thoughts are bothering you, maybe there's a strong pain instead, or maybe some abnormal mood is developing—whatever is happening, you have to look right in, look all the way in to the sensation of the mind. Once you have a sense of the empty mind, then if there's any disturbance, any sense of irritation, you'll know that the knowledge giving rise to it is wrong knowledge. Right knowledge will immediately take over, and the wrong knowledge will disband.

In order to hold continuously to this foundation of knowing, you first have to exercise restraint over the mind at the same time that you focus your attention and contemplate the phenomena of stress and pain. Keep this up until the mind can maintain its stance in the clear emptiness of the heart. If you can do this all the way to the end, the final disbanding of suffering will occur right there, right where the mind is empty.

But you have to keep practicing at this continuously. Whenever pain arises, regardless of whether it's strong or not, don't label it or give it any meaning. If pleasure arises, don't label it as *your* pleasure. Just keep letting it go, and the mind will gain release—empty of all clinging or attachment to "selfness." You have to apply all your mindfulness and energy to this at all times.

You should see yourself as fortunate that you're lying here ill, contemplating pain, for you have the opportunity to develop the Path in full measure, gaining insight and letting things go. Nobody has a better opportunity than you do right now. People running around engaged in their affairs are really no match for you, even if they say their minds are disengaged. A person lying ill in bed has the opportunity to develop insight with every in-and-out breath. It's a sign that you haven't wasted your birth as a human being, because you're practicing the teachings of the Lord Buddha to the point where you gain clear knowledge into the true nature of things in and of themselves.

The true nature of things, on the outer level, refers to the phenomenon of the present, the process of change in the five aggregates. You decipher their code again and again until you get disenchanted with them, lose your taste for them, and let them go. When the mind is in this state, the next step is to contemplate it skillfully to see how it's empty, all the way to the ultimate emptiness—the kind of emptiness that goes clearly into the true nature deep inside, where there's no concocting of thoughts, no arising, no passing away, no changing at all.

When you correctly see the nature of things on the outer level, and it's entirely clear to you, the mind will let go, let go. That's when you automatically see clearly what lies on the inner level—empty of all cycling through birth and death, with nothing concocted at all—the emptiest extreme of emptiness, with no labels, no meanings, no clinging or attachment. All I ask is that you see this clearly within your own mind.

The ordinary emptiness of the mind is useful on one level, but that's not all there is. True emptiness is empty until it reaches the true nature of things on the inner level—something really worth ferreting out, really worth coming to know.

This is something you have to know for yourself. There are really no words to describe it, but we can talk about it by way of guidance, because it may happen that ultimately you let go of everything, in what's called disbanding without trace.

The mind's point of disbanding without trace, if you keep developing insight every day, every moment, will happen on its own. The mind will know on its own. So don't let the mind bother itself by getting preoccupied with pleasure or pain. Relentlessly focus on penetrating into the mind itself.

Do you see how different this is from when you're running around strong and healthy, thinking about this, that, and the other thing? This is why there's no harm in having lots of pain. *The harm is in our stupidity* in giving labels and meanings to things. People tend to reflect on the fleeting nature of life when someone else grows sick or dies, but they rarely reflect on the fleeting nature of their own lives. Or else they reflect for just a moment and then forget all about it, getting completely involved in their preoccupations. They don't bring these truths inward, to reflect on the inconstancy occurring within themselves with every moment. They do this and that, think this and that, say this and that, and so they lose all perspective.

When you practice insight meditation, it's not something that you take a month or two off to do on a special retreat. That's not the real thing. It's no match for what you're doing right now, for here you can do it all day every day and all night, except when you sleep. Especially when the pain is strong, it's really good for your meditation, because it gives you the chance to know once and for all what inconstancy is like, what stress and suffering are like, what your inability to control things is like.

You have to find out right here, right in front of you, so don't try to avoid the pain. Practice insight so as to see the true nature of pain, its true nature as Dhamma, and then keep letting it go. If you do this, there's no way you can go wrong. This is the way to release from suffering.

And it's something you have to do before you die, you know, not something you wait to do when you die or are just about to die. It's something you simply keep on doing, keep on "insighting." When the disease lessens, "insight" it. When it grows heavy, "insight" it. If you keep on developing insight like this, the mind will get over its stupidity and delusion. In other words, things like craving and defilement won't dare hassle the mind the way they used to.

So give it your all—all your mindfulness, all your energy—now that you have the opportunity to practice the Dhamma. Let this be your last lifetime. Don't let there be anything born again. If you're born again, things will come back just as they are now. The same old stuff, over and over and over. Once there's birth, there has to be aging, illness, and death, in line with your defilements, forcing you to experience the good and bad results they keep churning out. It's a cycle of suffering. So the best thing is to gain release from birth. Don't let yourself want anything anymore, for all your wants fall in with what's inconstant, stressful, and not-self.

Wanting is simply a form of defilement and craving. You have to disband these things right at the instigator: the wanting that's nothing but craving for sensuality, craving for becoming, or craving for nonbecoming—the germs of birth in the heart. So contemplate at the right spot. Even though craving may be giving rise to birth at sensory contact, set your knowing right at the mind, right at consciousness itself, and let there just be *the knowing that lets go of knowing*. This is something to work at until you've mastered it.

The knowing that lets go of knowing is very beneficial. There's no getting stuck, no grabbing hold of your knowledge or views. If the knowledge is right, you let it go. If the knowledge is wrong, you let it go. This is called knowing the letting go of knowing without getting entangled. This kind of knowing keeps the mind from latching onto whatever arises. As soon as you know something, you've let it go. As soon as you know something, you've let it go. The mind just keeps on staying empty—empty of mental fabrications and thoughts, empty of every sort of illusion that could affect the mind. It quickly sees through them and lets them go, knows and lets go, without holding on to anything. All it has left is the emptiness.

You've already seen results from your practice, step by step, from contemplating things and letting them go, letting go even of the thought that *you* are the one in pain, that *you* are the one who's dying. The pain and the dying are an affair of the aggregates, pure and simple. When this knowledge is clear and sure—that it's not "my" affair, there's no "me" in there—there's just an empty mind, empty of any label for itself. This is the nature of the mind free of the germs that used to make it assume this and that. They're dead now, those germs, because we've contemplated them. We've let go. We've set our knowing right at the mind and let go of whatever knowing has arisen, to the point where the mind is empty, clear, in and of itself.

Consciousness, when you're aware of it inwardly, arises and passes away by its very own nature. There's no real essence to it— this is what you see when you look at the elemental property of consciousness *(viññāṇa-dhātu)*, pure and simple. When it's not involved with physical or mental phenomena, it's simply aware of itself—aware pure and simple. That's called the mind pure and simple, or the property of consciousness pure and simple, and it lets go of itself. When you're told to know and to let go of the knowing, it means to know the consciousness that senses things and then lets go of itself.

As for the aggregate of consciousness *(viññāṇa-khandha)*, that's a troublemaking consciousness. The germs that keep piling things on lie in this kind of consciousness, which wants to hang on to a sense of self. Even though it can let go of physical pain, or of physical and mental events in general, it still hangs on to a sense of self.

So when you're told to know the letting go of knowing, it means to let go of this kind of consciousness, to the point where consciousness has no label for itself. That's when it's empty. If you understand this, or can straighten out the heart and mind from this angle, there won't be anything left. Pain, suffering, stress—all your preoccupations—will become entirely meaningless. There will be no sense of good or bad or anything at all. Dualities will no longer be able to have an effect. If you know in this way—the knowing that lets go of knowing, consciousness pure and simple—it prevents any possible fashioning of the mind.

The dualities that fashion good and bad—there's really nothing to them. They arise, and that's all there is to them; they disband, and that's all there is to them. So now we come to know the affairs of the dualities that fashion the mind or consciousness into endless cycles. When you know the knowing that lets go of knowing, right at consciousness itself, dualities have no more meaning. There's no more latching onto the labels of good and bad, pleasure and pain, true and false, or whatever. You just keep on letting go.

Even this knowing that lets go of knowing has no label for itself such as "I know" or "I see." But this lies a little deep. It's something that you have to make an effort to see clearly and rightly. You have to keep looking in a shrewd way. The shrewdness of your looking is very important, for only that can lead to awakening. Your knowledge has to be shrewd, skillful. *Make sure that it's shrewd and skillful.* Otherwise your knowledge of the true nature of things—on the inner or outer levels—won't be clear. It'll get stuck on the elementary levels of emptiness, labeling and latching onto them in a way that just keeps piling things on. That kind of emptiness simply can't compare with this kind—the knowing that lets go of knowing right at consciousness pure and simple. Make sure that this kind of knowing keeps going continuously. If you slip for a moment, just get right back to it. You'll see that when you don't latch onto labels and meanings, thoughts of good and bad will just come to a stop. They'll disband. So when the Buddha tells us to see the world as empty, this is the way we see.

The emptiness lies in the fact that the mind doesn't give meaning to things, doesn't fashion things, doesn't cling. It's empty right at this kind of mind. Once you're correctly aware of this kind of empty mind, you'll no longer get carried away by anything at all. But if you don't really focus down like this, there will only be a little smattering of emptiness, and then you'll find yourself getting distracted by this and that, spoiling the emptiness. That kind of emptiness is emptiness in confusion. You're still caught up in confusion because you haven't contemplated down to the deeper levels. You simply play around with emptiness, that's all. The deeper levels of emptiness require that you focus in and keep on looking until you're thoroughly clear about the true nature of things, about the phenomenon of the present arising and disbanding right in front of you. This kind of mind doesn't get involved, doesn't latch onto meanings or labels.

If you see this kind of emptiness correctly, there are no more issues, no more labels for anything in this heap of physical and mental phenomena. When the time comes for it all to fall apart, there's nothing to get excited about, nothing to get upset about, for that's the way it has to go by its nature. *Only if we latch onto it will we suffer.*

The Dhamma is right here in our body and mind, simply that we don't see it—or we see it wrongly, latching on and making ourselves suffer. If we look at things with the eyes of mindfulness and discernment, what is there to make us suffer? Why is there any need to fear pain and death? Even if we do fear them, what do we accomplish? Physical and mental phenomena go their own way—inconstant, stressful, and beyond our control, all in their own way. So what business do we have in reaching out, latching on, thinking that their stress and pain is *our* stress and pain? If we understand that the latching on is what makes us suffer over and over again, with each and every breath, then all we have to do is let go and we'll see how there is release from suffering right before our very eyes.

So keep on looking, in the way I've described, right into the mind. But don't go labeling it as a "mind" or anything at all. Just let there be things as they are, in and of themselves, pure and simple. That's enough. You don't need to have any meanings or labels for anything at all. That will be the end of all suffering. When things disband in the ultimate way, they disband right at the point of the elemental property of consciousness free of the germs that will give rise to anything further. That's where everything comes to an end, with no more rebirth or redeath of any kind.

The practice is something you have to do for yourself. If you know things clearly and correctly with mindfulness and discernment, you have your tool, well-sharpened, in hand. If the mind is trained to be sharp, with mindfulness and discernment as its tool for contemplating itself, then defilement, craving, and attachment will keep getting weeded out and cleared away. You can see this from the amount you've already practiced. Aren't they already cleared away to some extent? The mind doesn't have to worry about anything, doesn't have to get involved with anything else. Let go of everything outside and then *keep* letting go until the mind lets go of itself. When you do this, how can you *not* see the great worth of the Dhamma?

So I ask that this mind empty of attachment, empty of any sense of self whatsoever, be clear to you. Then you'll see that it's nothing but Dhamma. Get it perfectly plain in your awareness that it's nothing but Dhamma. May this appear to you, as it is on its own, with each and every moment.

Listening to the Dhamma when the mind has already reached a basic level of emptiness is very useful. It's like an energizing tonic, for when we're sick, there's bound to be pain; but if we don't pay it any attention, it simply becomes an affair of the body, without involving the mind at all. Notice this as you're listening. When you listen to my words, the mind lets go of pain, leaving it to its own affairs. The mind is then empty.

Once the mind honestly sees the truth that all fabricated things are inconstant, it will have to let go of its attachments. The problem here is that we haven't yet really seen this, or haven't yet reflected on it in a skillful way. Once we do, though, the mind always grows radiant. Clear knowing immediately makes the mind radiant. So keep careful watch on things. Even if you don't see very much, just be aware of the mind as it maintains a balance in its basic level of neutrality and emptiness. Then it won't be able to fashion pains in the body into big issues, and you won't have to be attached to them.

So keep your awareness of the pain right at the level where it's no more than a mere sensation in the body. It can be the body's pain, but don't let the mind be in pain with it. If you *do* let the mind be in pain with it, the mind will pile things on, layer after layer. So the first step is to protect the mind, to let things go, then turn inward to look for the deepest, innermost part of your awareness and stay right there. *You don't have to get involved with the pains outside.* If you simply try to endure them, they may be too much for you to bear. So look for the aspect of the mind that lies deep within and you'll be able to put everything else aside.

Now, if the pains are the sort you can watch, make an effort to watch them. The mind will stay at its normal neutrality, calm with its own inner emptiness, watching each pain as it changes and passes. But if the pain is too extreme, then turn around and go back inside; for if you can't handle it, craving will work its way into the picture, push the pain away, and try to get some pleasure. This will keep piling on, piling on, putting the mind in a horrible turmoil.

So start out by solving the problem right at hand. If the pain is sudden and sharp, immediately turn around and focus all your attention on the mind. You don't want to have anything to do with the body, anything to do with the pains in the body. Don't look at them. Don't pay them any attention. Focus on staying with the innermost part of your awareness. Get to the point where you can see the pure state of mind that isn't in pain along with the body's pain, and keep it constantly clear.

Once this is constantly clear, then no matter how much pain there is in the body, it's simply an affair of mental and physical events. The mind, though, isn't involved. It puts all these things aside. It lets go.

When you're adept at this, it's a very useful skill, because the important things in life don't lie outside. They lie entirely within the mind. If we understand this properly, we won't have to go out and grab this or that. We won't have to latch onto anything at all—because if we do latch on, we simply cause ourselves needless suffering. The well-being of the mind lies at the point where it doesn't latch onto anything, where it doesn't want anything. That's where our well-being lies—the point where all suffering and stress disband right at the mind.

If we don't really understand things, though, the mind won't be willing to let things go. It will keep on holding tight, for it finds so much flavor in things outside. Whatever involves pain and stress, that's what it likes.

We have to focus on contemplating and looking. We have to see the illusions in the mind, the wrong knowledge and opinions that cover it up and keep us from seeing the aspect of the mind that's empty and still by its own internal nature. Focus on contemplating the opinions that give rise to the complicated attachments that bury the mind until it's in awful straits. See how mental events—feelings, perceptions, and thought-fabrications—condition the mind, condition the property of consciousness until it's in terrible shape.

This is why it's so important to ferret out the type of knowing that lets go of knowing—that knows the property of consciousness pure and simple when mental events haven't yet come in to condition it, or when it hasn't gone out to condition mental events. Right here is where things get really interesting—in particular, the thought-fabrications that condition consciousness. They come from ignorance, right? It's because of our not knowing, or our wrong knowing, that they're able to condition things.

So I ask you to focus on this ignorance, this not-knowing. If you can know the characteristics of not-knowing, this same knowledge will know both the characteristics of thought-fabrications as they go about their conditioning and how to disband them. This requires adroit contemplation because it's subtle and deep.

But no matter how subtle it may be, the fact that we've developed our mindfulness and discernment to this point means that we have to take an interest in it. If we don't, there's no way we can put an end to stress or gain release from it.

Or, if you want, you can approach it like this: Focus exclusively on the aspect of the mind that's constantly empty. If any preoccupations appear to it, be aware of the characteristics of bare sensation when forms make contact with the eye, or sounds with the ear, and so forth. There's a bare sensation, and then it disbands before it can have any such meaning as "good" or "bad." *If there's just the bare sensation that then disbands, there's no suffering.*

Be observant of the moment when forms make contact with the eye. With some things, if we're not interested in them, no feelings of liking or disliking arise. But if we get interested or feel that there's a meaning to the form, sound, smell, taste, or tactile sensation, you'll notice that as soon as you give a meaning to these things, attachment is already there.

If you stop to look, you'll see that attachment is subtle, because it's there even in the simple act of giving meaning. If you look in a superficial way, you won't see that it's attachment—even though that's what it is, but in a subtle way. *As soon as there's a meaning, there's already attachment.* This requires that you have to be good and observant—because in the contact at the eyes and ears that we take so much for granted, many sleights of hand happen all at once, which means that we aren't aware of the characteristics of the consciousness that knows each individual sensation. We have to be very observant if we want to know these things. If we aren't aware on this level, everything will be tied up in attachment. These things will keep sending their reports into the mind, conditioning and concocting all kinds of issues to leave the mind, or consciousness, in utter turmoil.

So if we want to look purely inside, we have to be very, very observant, because things inside are subtle, elusive, and sensitive. When the mind seems empty and neutral, that's when you really have to keep careful watch and control over it, so as to see clearly the sensation of receiving contact. There's contact pure and simple, then it disbands, and the mind is empty. Neutral and empty. Once you know this, you'll know what the mind is like when it isn't conditioned by the power of defilement, craving, and attachment. We can use this emptiness of the mind as our standard of comparison, and it will do us a world of good.

Ultimately, you'll see the emptiness of all sensory contacts, as in the Buddha's teaching that you should see the world as empty. What he meant is that you observe bare sensations as they simply arise and pass away, and you know what consciousness is like when it does nothing more than receive contact. If you can see this, the next step in the practice won't be difficult at all—because you've established neutrality right from the start. The act of receiving contact is no longer complicated. The mind no longer grabs hold of things, no longer feels any likes or dislikes. It's simply quiet and aware all around within itself at all times. If you can do this much, you find that you benefit from keeping things simple, from not concocting things through the power of defilement, craving, and attachment. Even just this much gets rid of lots of problems.

Then when you focus further in and see the nature of all phenomena that are known through sensory contact, you'll see that there's simply bare sensation with nothing at all worth getting attached to. If you look with the eyes of true mindfulness and discernment, you'll see emptiness—even though the world is full of things. The eye sees lots of forms, the ear hears lots of sounds, but the mind no longer gives them meanings. At the same time, things have no meanings in and of themselves.

The only important thing is the mind. *All issues come from the mind that goes out and gives things meanings* and gives rise to attachment, creating stress and suffering for itself. So you have to look until you see all the way through. Look outward until you see all the way out, and inward until you see all the way in, all the way until you penetrate inconstancy, stress, and not-selfness. See things as they are, in and of themselves, in line with their own nature, without any meanings or attachments. Then there won't be any issues. The mind will be empty—clean and bright—without your having to do anything to it.

Because the mind has the virus of ignorance or of the craving that gives rise to things easily, you can't be careless. In the beginning, you have to supervise things carefully so that you can see the craving that arises at the moment of contact—say, when there's a feeling of pain. If you don't label it as meaning *your* pain, craving won't get too much into the act. But if you do give it that meaning, then there will be the desire to push the pain away or to have pleasure come in its place.

All this, even though we've never gotten anything true and dependable from desire. The pleasure we get from desire doesn't last. It fools us and then changes into something else. Pain fools us and then changes into something else. But these changes keep piling up and getting very complicated in the mind, and this is what keeps the mind ignorant. It has been conditioned in so many ways that it gets confused, deluded, dark, and smoldering.

All kinds of things are smoldering in here. That's why the principle of the knowing that lets go of knowing is such an important tool. Whatever comes at you, the knowing that lets go of knowing is enough to get you through. It takes care of everything. If you let it slip, simply get back to the same sort of knowing. See for yourself how far it will take you, how neutral and empty it keeps the mind.

You can come to see this bit by bit. When the mind isn't involved with very much, when it's at a basic level of normalcy—empty, quiet—watch it and analyze it carefully. Don't let it lapse into a state of oblivious indifference, or else it will lose its balance. If you're in an oblivious state, then as soon as there's contact at any of the sense doors, as soon as a feeling appears, there's sure to be attachment or craving. You have to keep watching how the mind changes, how it behaves at every moment. As soon as your mindfulness lapses, get back immediately to your original knowing. We're all bound to have lapses—all of us—because the fermentation of ignorance, the most important of the fermentations, is still there in the mind.

This is why we have to keep working at our watchfulness, our investigation, our focused awareness, so that we keep getting clearer and clearer. Ripen your mindfulness and discernment continuously.

Once they're ripe enough for you to know things skillfully, you'll be able to disband the defilements the very minute they appear. As soon as you begin feeling likes and dislikes, you can deal with them before they amount to anything. This makes things a lot easier. If you let them loose so that they condition the mind, making it irritated, murky, and muddled to the point where it affects your words and actions, then you're in terrible straits, falling into hell in this very lifetime.

The practice of the Dhamma requires us to be ingenious and circumspect right at the mind. The defilements are always ready to flatter us, to work their way into our favor. If we aren't skillful, if we don't know how to keep the mind under careful supervision, we'll be no match for them—for they are so many. But if we keep the mind well supervised, the defilements will be afraid of us—afraid of our mindfulness and discernment, afraid of our awareness.

Notice when the mind is empty, aware all around, with no attachments to anything at all: The defilements will hide out—quiet—as if they weren't there at all. But as soon as mindfulness slips, even just a little, they spring right up. If you recognize them the moment they spring up, they'll disband right there. This is a very useful skill to have. But if we let them get to the point where they turn into issues, they'll be hard to disband. That's when you have to stick with the fight and not give up.

Whatever happens, start out by sticking with it—*not simply out of endurance, but to examine it,* to see what it's like, how it changes, how it passes away. We stick with things so that we can see through their deceits: the way they arise, persist, and disband on their own. If they disband while we're examining them and seeing their deceitfulness, we can be done with them for good. This will leave the mind in a state of freedom and independence, empty entirely within itself.

If you can learn to see through things the moment they arise—and keep having your own little instants of Awakening—your awareness will keep getting brighter, stronger, and more expansive.

So work at them—these little instants of understanding—and eventually, when things come together in an appropriate way, there will be the moment where there's the instantaneous cutting through of defilements and mental fermentations once and for all. When that happens, then: *nibbāna.* No more taking birth. But if you have yet to reach that point, just keep sharpening your knives: your mindfulness and discernment. If they're dull, they won't be able to cut anything all the way through, but whatever shape they're in, keep cutting through bit by bit whatever you can.

I urge you to keep at this. Keep examining and investigating the mind from every angle until you reach the point where everything is totally clear and you can let go of everything, with the realization that nothing in the five aggregates or in physical and mental phenomena is "me" or "mine." Keep trying to let go, and that will be enough. Each moment, when they're taking care of you here in the hospital, do what has to be done for your illness, but make sure that there's this separate, special awareness exclusive to the mind—this knowing that simply lets go of itself. That will end all your problems right there.

READING THE MIND

DISCERNMENT VERSUS SELF-DECEPTION

It's important that we discuss the steps of the practice in training the mind, for the mind has all sorts of deceptions by which it fools itself. If you aren't skillful in investigating and seeing through them, they are very difficult to overcome even if you're continually mindful to keep watch over the mind. You have to make an effort to contemplate these things at all times. Mindfulness on its own won't be able to give rise to any real knowledge. At best, it can give you only a little protection against the effects of sensory contact. If you don't make a focused contemplation, the mind won't be able to give rise to any knowledge within itself at all.

This is why you have to train yourself to be constantly aware all around. When you come to know anything for what it really is, there's nothing but letting go, letting go. On the beginning level, this means the mind won't give rise to any unwise or unskillful thoughts. It will simply stop to watch, stop to know within itself. If there's anything you have to think about, keep your thoughts on the themes of inconstancy, stress, and not-self. You have to keep the mind thinking and labeling solely in reference to these sorts of themes, for if your thinking and labeling are right, you'll come to see things rightly. If you go the opposite way and label things wrongly, you'll see things wrongly as well. This keeps the mind completely hidden from itself.

Now, when thoughts or labels arise in the mind, then if you focus on watching them closely, you'll see that they're sensations—sensations of arising and disbanding, changeable, unreliable, and illusory. If you don't make an effort to keep a focused watch on them, you'll fall for the deceptions of thought-fabrication. In other words, the mind gives rise to memories of the past and fashions issues dealing with the past, but if you're aware of what's going on in time, you'll see that they're all illusory. There's no real truth to them at all. Even the meanings the mind gives to good and bad sensory contacts at the moment they occur: If you carefully observe and contemplate them, you'll see that they're all deceptive. There's no real truth to them. But ignorance and delusion latch onto them, and this drives the mind around in circles. It doesn't know what's what—how these things arise, persist, and disband—so it latches onto them and gets itself deceived on many, many levels. If you don't stop and focus, there's no way you can see through these things.

But if the mind keeps its balance, stopping to watch and know itself, it realizes these things for what they are. When it does that, it lets them go automatically without being attached. This is the knowledge that comes with true mindfulness and discernment. It knows and lets go; it doesn't cling. No matter what appears—good or bad, pleasure or pain—when the mind knows, it doesn't cling. *When it doesn't cling, there's no stress or suffering.* You have to keep hammering away at this point. When it doesn't cling, the mind can stay at normalcy: empty, undisturbed, and quiet. But if it doesn't read and know itself in this way, it will fall for the deceits of defilement and craving. It will conjure up all sorts of complex and complicated things that it will then have a hard time seeing through, for they have their ways of playing up to the mind to keep it attached to them, all of which is simply a matter of the mind's falling for the deceits of the defilements and cravings within itself. The fact that it isn't acquainted with itself—doesn't know how mental states arise and disband and take on objects—means that it loses itself in its many, many attachments.

There's nothing as hard to keep watch of as the mind, because it's so accustomed to wrong views and wrong opinions. This is what keeps it hidden from itself. But thanks to the teachings of the Buddha, we can gain knowledge into the mind, or into consciousness with its many layers and intricacies, which when you look into it deeply, you'll find to be empty—empty of any meaning in and of itself.

This is an emptiness that can appear clearly within consciousness. Even though it's hidden and profound, we can see into it by looking inward in a way that's quiet and still. The mind stops to watch, to know within itself. As for sensory contacts—sights, sounds, smells, tastes, and that sort of thing—it isn't interested, because it's intent on looking into consciousness pure and simple, to see what arises in there and how it generates issues. Sensations, thoughts, labels for pleasure and pain and so forth, are all natural phenomena that change as soon as they're sensed—and they're very refined. If you view them as being about this or that matter, you won't be able to know them for what they are. The more intricate the meanings you give them, the more lost you become—lost in the whorls of the cycle of rebirth.

The cycle of rebirth and the processes of thought-fabrication are one and the same thing. As a result, we whirl around and around, lost in many, many levels of thought-fabrication, not just one. The knowledge that would read the heart can't break through, for it whirls around and around in these very same thought-fabrications, giving them meaning in terms of this or that, and then latching onto them. If it labels them as good, it latches onto them as good. If it labels them as bad, it latches onto them as bad. This is why the mind stays entirely in the whorls of the cycle of rebirth, the cycle of thought-fabrication.

To see these things clearly requires the effort to stop and watch, to stop and know *in an appropriate way,* in a way that's just right. At the same time, you have to use your powers of observation. *That's* what will enable you to read your own consciousness in a special way. Otherwise, if you latch onto the issues of thoughts and labels, they'll keep you spinning around. So you have to stop and watch, stop and know clearly by focusing—*focusing on the consciousness in charge.* That way your knowledge will become skillful.

Ultimately, you'll see that there's nothing at all—just the arising and disbanding occurring every moment in emptiness. If there's no attachment, there are no issues. There's simply the natural phenomenon of arising and disbanding. But because we don't see things simply as natural phenomena, we see them as being true and latch onto them as self, as good or bad, and as all sorts of complicated things. This keeps us spinning around without knowing how to find a way out or what to let go of—we just don't know. When we don't know, we're like a person who wanders into a jungle and can't find the way out.

Actually what we have to let go of lies right smack in front of us, where the mind fashions things and gives them meanings so that it doesn't know the characteristics of arising and disbanding, pure and simple. If you can simply keep watching and knowing, without any need for meanings, thoughts, imaginings—simply watching the process itself—there won't be any issues. There's just the phenomenon of the present: arising, persisting, disbanding, arising, persisting, disbanding.... There's no special trick to this, but you have to stop and watch, stop and know within yourself *at every moment.* Don't let your awareness stream away from awareness to outside preoccupations. Gather it in so it can know itself clearly—that there's nothing in there worth latching onto. It's all a mass of deceit.

To know just this much is very useful for seeing the truth inside yourself. You'll see that consciousness is empty of any self. When you look at physical phenomena, you'll see them as elements, as empty of self. You'll see mental phenomena as empty of self, as elements of consciousness. And you'll see that if there's no attachment, no latching on, there's no suffering or stress.

So even if there's thinking going on in the mind, simply watch it, let it go, and its cycling will slow down. Fewer and fewer thought-fabrications will occur. Even if the mind doesn't stop completely, it will form fewer and fewer thoughts. You'll be able to stop and watch, stop and know more and more. And this way, you'll come to see the tricks and deceits of thought-fabrication, mental labels, pleasure and pain, and so on. You'll be able to know that there's really nothing inside—that the reason you were deluded into latching onto things was your ignorance, and that you made yourself suffer right there in that very ignorance.

So you have to focus on one point, one thing. Focusing on many things won't do. Keep mindfulness in place: stopping, knowing, seeing. Don't let it run out after thoughts and labels. But knowing in this way requires that you make the effort to stay focused—focused on seeing clearly, not just focused on making the mind still. Focus on seeing clearly. Look inside to see clearly, and contemplate how to let go. The mind will become empty in line with its nature in a way that you'll know exclusively within.

A DIFFERENCE IN THE KNOWING

What can we do to see the aggregates—this mass of suffering and stress—so clearly that we can cut attachment for them out of the mind? Why is it that people studying to be doctors can know everything in the body—intestines, liver, kidneys, and all—down to the details, and yet don't develop any dispassion or disenchantment for it—why? Why is it that undertakers can spend their time with countless corpses and yet not gain any insight at all? This shows that insight is hard to attain. If there's no mindfulness and discernment to see things clearly for what they are, knowledge is simply a passing fancy. It doesn't sink in. The mind keeps latching onto its attachments.

But if the mind can gain true insight to the point where it can relinquish its attachments, it can gain the paths and fruitions leading to *nibbāna.* This shows that there's a difference in the knowing. It's not that we have to know all the details like modern-day surgeons. All we have to know is that the body is composed of the four physical elements plus the elements of space and consciousness. If we *really* know just this much, we've reached the paths and their fruitions, while those who know all the details, to the point where they can perform fine surgery, don't reach any transcendent attainments at all.

So let's analyze the body into its elements so as to know them thoroughly. If we do, then when there are changes in the body and mind, there won't be too much clinging. If we don't, our attachments will be fixed and strong and will lead to future states of being and birth.

Now that we have the opportunity, we should contemplate the body and take it apart to get down to the details. Take the five basic meditation objects—hair of the head, hair of the body, nails, teeth, and skin—and look at them carefully one at a time. You don't have to take on all five, you know. Focus on the hair of the head to see that it belongs to the earth element, to see that its roots are soaked in blood and lymph under the skin. It's unattractive in terms of its color, its smell, and where it dwells. If you analyze and contemplate these things, you won't be deluded into regarding them as *yours*: your hair, your nails, your teeth, your skin.

All of these parts are composed of the earth element mixed in with water, wind, and fire. If they were purely earth they wouldn't last, because every part of the body has to be composed of all four elements for it to be a body. And then there's a mental phenomenon, the mind, in charge. These are things that follow in line with nature—the arising, changing, and disbanding of physical and mental phenomena—but we latch onto them, seeing the body as ours, the mental phenomena as us: It's all us and ours. If we don't see these things for what they are, we'll do nothing but cling to them.

This is what meditation is: seeing things clearly for what they are. It's not a matter of switching from topic to topic, for that would simply ensure that you wouldn't know a thing. But our inner character, under the sway of ignorance and delusion, doesn't like examining itself repeatedly. It keeps finding other issues to get in the way, so that we think constantly about other things. This is why we stay so ignorant and foolish.

Then why is it that we can know other things? Because they fall in line with what craving wants. To see things clearly for what they are would be to abandon craving, so it finds ways of keeping things hidden. It keeps changing, bringing in new things, keeping us fooled, so that we study and think about nothing but matters that add to the mind's suffering and stress. That's all that craving wants. As for the kind of study that would end the stress and suffering in the mind, it's always getting in craving's way.

This is why the mind is always wanting to shift to new things to know, new things to fall for. And this is why it's always becoming attached. So when it doesn't really know itself, you have to make a real effort to see the truth that the things within it aren't you or yours. Don't let the mind stop short of this knowledge. Make this a law within yourself. If the mind doesn't know the truths of inconstancy, stress, and not-self within itself, it won't gain release from suffering. Its knowledge will be worldly knowledge; it will follow a worldly path. It won't reach the paths and fruition leading to *nibbāna*.

So this is where the worldly and the transcendent part ways. If you comprehend inconstancy, stress, and not-self to the ultimate degree, that's the transcendent. If you don't get down to their details, you're still on the worldly level.

The Buddha has many teachings, but this is what they all come down to. The important principles of the practice—the four establishings of mindfulness, the four Noble Truths—all come down to these characteristics of inconstancy, stress, and not-selfness. If you try to learn too many principles, you'll end up with no clear knowledge of the truth as it is. *If you focus on knowing just a little, you'll end up with more true insight than if you try knowing a lot.* It's through wanting to know too many things that we end up deluded. We wander around in our deluded knowledge, thinking and labeling things, *but knowledge that is focused and specific, when it really knows, is absolute.* It keeps hammering away at one point. There's no need to know a lot of things, for when you really know one thing, everything converges right there.

THE BALANCED WAY

In practicing the Dhamma, if you don't foster a balance between concentration and discernment, you'll end up going wild in your thinking. If there's too much working at discernment, you'll go wild in your thinking. But if there's too much concentration, the mind just stays still and undisturbed without coming to any knowledge. So you have to keep discernment and stillness in balance. Don't let there be too much of one or the other. Try to get them just right. That's when you'll be able to see things clearly all the way through. Otherwise you'll stay as deluded as ever. You may want to gain discernment into too many things—and as a result your thinking goes wild. Some people keep wondering why discernment never arises in their practice, but when it does arise they really go off on a tangent. Their thinking goes wild, all out of bounds.

So when you practice, you have to observe in your meditation how you can make the mind still. Once it does grow still, it tends to get stuck there. Or it may become empty, without any knowledge of anything: quiet, disengaged, at ease for a while, but without any discernment to accompany it. But if you *can* get discernment to accompany your concentration, that's when you'll really benefit. You'll see things all the way through and be able to let them go. If you're too heavy on the side of either discernment or stillness, you can't let go. The mind may come to know this or that, but it latches onto its knowledge. Then it knows still other things and latches onto them, too. Or else it simply stays perfectly quiet and latches onto *that.*

It's not easy to keep your practice on the Middle Way. If you don't use your powers of observation, it's especially hard. The mind will keep falling for things, sometimes right, sometimes wrong, because it doesn't observe what's going on. This isn't the path to letting go. It's a path to getting stuck, caught up in things. If you don't know what it's stuck and caught up in, you'll remain foolish and deluded. So make an effort at focused contemplation until you see clearly into inconstancy, stress, and not-self. This, without a doubt, will stop every moment of suffering and stress.

THE USES OF EQUANIMITY

The sensations of the mind are subtle and very volatile. Sometimes passion or irritation can arise independently of sensory contact, simply in line with one's character. For instance, there are times when the mind is perfectly normal and all of a sudden there's irritation—or there's a desire to form thoughts and get engrossed in feelings of pain, pleasure, or equanimity. We have to contemplate these three kinds of feeling to see how they're inconstant, always changing, and stressful, so that the mind won't go and get engrossed in them. This business of getting engrossed is subtle. It keeps us from knowing what's what; it's delusion pure and simple. Being engrossed in feelings of pleasure is relatively easy to detect, but being engrossed in feelings of equanimity, that's hard to notice—if the mind is at equanimity in an oblivious way. This oblivious equanimity keeps us from seeing anything clearly.

So you have to focus on seeing feelings simply as feelings and pull the mind out of its infatuation with equanimity. When there's a feeling of equanimity as the mind gathers and settles down, use that feeling of equanimity in concentration as the basis for probing into inconstancy, stress, and not-self—for this equanimity in concentration at the fourth level of absorption *(jhāna)* is the basis for liberating insight. Simply make sure that you don't get attached to the absorption.

If you get the mind to grow still in equanimity without focusing on gaining insight, you achive only a temporary state of concentration. So you have to focus on gaining clear insight either into inconstancy, into stress, or into not-selfness. That's when you'll be able to uproot your attachments. If the mind gets into a state of oblivious equanimity, it's still carrying fuel inside it. Then as soon as there's sensory contact, it flares up into attachment. So we have to follow the principles the Buddha laid down: Focus the mind into a state of absorption and then focus on gaining clear insight into the three characteristics. The proper way to practice is not to let yourself get stuck on this level or that—*and no matter what insights you may gain, don't go thinking that you've gained Awakening.* Keep looking. Keep focusing and see if there are any further changes in the mind, and if there are, see the stress and the not-selfness of those changes. If you can know in this way, the mind will rise above feeling, no longer entangled in this level or that level—all of which are simply matters of speculation.

The important thing is that you try to see clearly. Even when the mind is fabricating all sorts of objects in a real turmoil, see these objects as illusory. Then stay still and watch their disbanding. See clearly that there's really nothing to them. They all disband. All that remains is the empty mind—the mind maintaining its balance in normalcy. Focus on examining *that*.

There are many levels of examining the diseases in the mind, not just one. If you come up with a genuine insight, don't stop there—and don't get excited about seeing things you never saw before. Just keep contemplating the theme of inconstancy in everything, without latching on, and then you'll come to even more penetrating insights.

So keep focusing until the mind stops, until it reaches the stage of absorption called purity of mindfulness and equanimity. See what pure mindfulness is like. As for the feeling of equanimity, that's an affair of concentration. It's what the mindfulness depends on so that it too can reach equanimity. This is the stage where we consolidate our awareness in order to come in and know the mind. Get the mind centered, at equanimity, and then probe in and contemplate. That's when you'll be able to see.

A GLOB OF TAR

An important but subtle point in our practice is that we continue to fall for pleasant feelings, because feelings are illusory on many levels. We don't realize that they're changeable and unreliable. Instead of offering pleasure, they offer us nothing but stress—yet we're still addicted to them.

This business of feeling is thus a subtle matter. Please contemplate it carefully, this business of latching onto feelings of pleasure, pain, or equanimity. You have to contemplate it and see it clearly. And you have to experiment more than you may want to with pain. When there are feelings of physical pain or mental distress, the mind will struggle because it doesn't like pain. But when pain turns to pleasure, the mind likes it and is content with it, so it keeps on playing with feeling, even though, as we've said, feeling is inconstant, stressful, and not really ours. But the mind doesn't see this. All it sees are feelings of pleasure, and it wants them.

Try looking into how feeling gives rise to craving. It's because we want pleasant feeling that craving whispers—whispers right there at the feeling. If you observe carefully, you'll see that this is very important, for this is where the paths and fruitions leading to *nibbāna* are attained, right here at feeling and craving. If we can extinguish the craving in feeling, that's *nibbāna*.

In the *Soḷasa Pañhā (Sutta Nipāta V)*, the Buddha said that defilement is like a wide and deep flood, but he then summarized the practice of crossing this flood simply as abandoning craving in every action. Now, right here at feeling is where we can practice abandoning craving, for the way we relish the flavor of feeling has many ramifications. This is where many of us get deceived, because we don't see feeling as inconstant. We want it to be constant. We want pleasant feelings to be constant. As for pain, we don't want it to be constant, but no matter how much we try to push it away, we still latch onto it.

We have to focus on feeling so that we can abandon craving right there in the feeling. If you don't focus here, the other paths you follow will simply proliferate. So bring the practice close to home. When the mind gains a sense of stillness or a feeling of pleasure or equanimity, try to see how the pleasure or equanimity is inconstant, how it's not you or yours. When you can do this, you'll stop relishing that particular feeling. You can stop right there, right where the mind relishes the flavor of feeling and gives rise to craving. This is why the mind has to be fully aware of itself—all around, at all times—in its focused contemplation to see feeling as empty of self.

This business of liking and disliking feelings is a disease hard to detect, because our intoxication with feelings is so very strong. Even with the sensations of peace and emptiness in the mind, we're still infatuated with feeling. Feelings on the crude level—the violent and stressful ones that come with defilement—are easy to detect. But when the mind grows still—steady, cool, bright—we're still addicted to feeling. We want these feelings of pleasure or equanimity. We enjoy them. Even on the level of firm concentration or meditative absorption, there's attachment to the feeling.

This is the subtle magnetic pull of craving, which paints and plasters things over. It's hard to detect because craving is always whispering, "I want nothing but pleasant feelings." This is very important, for this virus of craving is what causes us to be continually reborn.

So explore how craving paints and plasters things, how it causes desires to form—the desires to get this or take that—and how its addictive flavor makes it hard for you to pull away. You have to see how craving fastens the mind so firmly to feelings that you never weary of sensuality or of pleasant feelings, no matter what kind. If you don't see clearly that the mind is stuck right here at feeling and craving, it will keep you from gaining release.

We're stuck on feeling like a monkey stuck in a tar trap. They take a glob of tar and put it where a monkey will get its hand stuck in it and, in trying to pull free, the monkey gets its other hand, both feet, and finally its mouth stuck, too. Consider this. Whatever we do, we end up stuck right here at feeling and craving. We can't separate them out. We can't wash them off. If we don't grow weary of craving, we're like the monkey stuck in tar. So if we're intent on freeing ourselves in the footsteps of the arahants, we have to focus specifically on feeling until we can succeed in freeing ourselves from it. Even with painful feelings, we have to practice—for if we're afraid of pain and always try to change it to pleasure, we'll end up even more ignorant than before.

This is why we have to be brave in experimenting with pain—both physical pain and mental distress. When it arises in full measure, like a house afire, can we let go of it? We have to know both sides of feeling. When it's hot and burning, how can we deal with it? When it's cool and refreshing, how can we see through it? We have to make an effort to focus on both sides, contemplating until we know how to let go. Otherwise we won't know anything, for all we want is the cool side, the cooler the better...and when this is the case, how can we expect to gain release from the cycle of rebirth?

Nibbāna is the extinguishing of craving, and yet we like to stick with craving—so how can we expect to get anywhere? We'll stay right here in the world, right here with stress and suffering, for craving is a sticky sap. If there's no craving, there's nothing: no stress, no rebirth. But we have to watch out for it. It's a sticky sap, a glob of tar, a dye that's hard to wash out.

So don't let yourself get carried away with feeling. The crucial part of the practice lies here.

WHEN CONVENTIONAL TRUTHS COLLAPSE

In making yourself quiet, you have to be quiet on all fronts—quiet in your deeds, quiet in your words, quiet in your mind. Only then will you be able to contemplate what's going on inside yourself. If you aren't quiet, you'll become involved in external affairs and end up having too much to do and too much to say. This will keep your awareness or mindfulness from holding steady and firm. You have to stop doing, saying, or thinking anything that isn't necessary. That way your mindfulness will be able to develop continuously. Don't let yourself get involved in too many outside things.

In training your mindfulness to be continuous so that it will enable you to contemplate yourself, you have to be observant. When there's sensory contact, can the mind stay continuously undisturbed and at normalcy? Or does it run out into liking and disliking? Being observant in this way will enable you to read yourself, to know yourself. If mindfulness is firmly established, the mind won't waver. If it's not yet firm, the mind will waver in the form of liking and disliking. You have to be wary of even the slightest wavering. Don't let yourself think that the slight waverings are unimportant, or else they'll become habitual.

Being heedful means that you have to watch out for the details, the little things, the tiny flaws that arise in the mind. If you can do this, you'll be able to keep your mind protected—which is so much better than giving all your attention to the worthless affairs of the outside world. So really try to be careful. Don't get entangled in sensory contact. This is something you have to work at mastering. If you focus yourself exclusively in the area of the mind like this, you'll be able to contemplate feelings in all their details. You'll be able to see them clearly and let them go.

So focus your practice right at feelings of pleasure, pain, and neither-pleasure-nor-pain. Contemplate how to leave them alone, simply as feelings, without relishing them—*for if you relish feelings, that's craving.* Desires for this and that will seep in and influence the mind so that it gets carried away with inner and outer feelings. This is why you have to be quiet—quiet in a way that doesn't let the mind become attached to the flavors of feelings, quiet in a way that uproots their influence.

The desire for pleasure is like a virus deep in our character. What we're doing here is getting the mind to stop taking in pleasant feelings and pushing out painful ones. It's because we're addicted to taking in pleasant feelings that we dislike painful feelings and push them away. So don't let the mind love pleasure and resist pain. Let it be undisturbed by both. Give it a try. If the mind can let go of feelings so that it's above pleasure, pain, and indifference, that means it's not stuck on feeling. And then try to observe how it can *stay* unaffected by feelings. This is something you have to work at mastering in order to release your grasp on feelings once and for all, so that you won't latch onto physical pain or mental distress as being you or yours.

If you don't release your grasp on feeling, you'll stay attached to it, in both its physical and mental forms. If there's the pleasure of physical ease, you'll be attracted to it. As for the purely mental feeling of pleasure, that's something you'll really want, you'll really love. And then you'll be attracted to the mental perceptions and labels that accompany the pleasure, the thought-fabrications and even the consciousness that accompany the pleasure. You'll latch onto all of these things as you or yours.

So analyze physical and mental pleasure. Take them apart and contemplate how to let them go. Don't fool yourself into relishing them. As for pain, don't push it away. *Let pain simply be pain; let pleasure simply be pleasure.* Let them simply fall into the category of feelings. Don't go thinking that *you* feel pleasure, that *you* feel pain If you can let go of feeling in this way, you'll be able to gain release from suffering and stress *because you'll be above and beyond feeling.* Then, when aging, illness, and death come, you won't latch onto the notion that *you* are aging, *you* are ill, *you* are dying. You'll be able to release these things from your grasp.

If you can contemplate purely in these terms—that the five aggregates are inconstant, stressful, and not-self—you won't enter into them and latch onto them as "you" or "yours." If you don't analyze them in this way, you'll be trapped in dying. Even your bones, skin, flesh, and so forth will become "yours." This is why we're taught to contemplate death—so that we can make ourselves aware that death doesn't mean that *we* die. You have to contemplate until you really know this. Otherwise, you'll stay trapped right there. You must make yourself sensitive in a way that sees clearly how your bones, flesh, and skin are empty of any self. That way you won't latch onto them. If you still latch onto them, you haven't really seen into their inconstancy, stress, and not-selfness.

When you see the bones of animals, they don't have much meaning, but when you see the bones of people, your perception labels them: "That's a person's skeleton. That's a person's skull." If there are a lot of them, they can really scare you. When you see the picture of a skeleton or of anything that shows the inconstancy and not-selfness of the body, you'll get stuck there, at the level of skeleton and bones, unless you see clear through it. Actually, there are no bones at all. Bones are empty, nothing but elements. If you penetrate into them, you'll see that they're elements. Otherwise, you'll get stuck at the level of skeleton. And since you haven't seen through it, it can make you upset. This shows that you haven't penetrated into the Dhamma. You're stuck at the outer shell because you haven't analyzed things into their elements.

Days and nights go by, but they're not the only things that go by. The body constantly decays and falls apart, too. The body decays bit by bit, but we don't realize it. Only after it's decayed a lot—when the hair has gone gray and the teeth fall out—do we realize that it's old. This is knowledge on a crude and really blatant level. But as for the gradual decaying that goes on quietly inside, we aren't aware of it.

As a result, we cling to the body as being us—every single part of it. Its eyes are *our* eyes, the sights they see are the things *we* see, the sensation of seeing is something *we* sense. We don't see these things as elements. Actually, the element of vision and the element of form make contact. The awareness of the contact is the element of consciousness: the mental phenomenon that senses sights, sounds, smells, tastes, tactile sensations, and ideas. This we don't realize, which is why we latch onto everything—eyes, ears, nose, tongue, body, intellect—as being us or ours. Then, when the body decays, we feel that *we* are growing old; when it dies and mental phenomena stop, we feel that *we* die.

Once you've taken the elements apart, though, there's nothing. These things lose their meaning on their own. *They're simply physical and mental elements, without any illness or death.* If you don't penetrate into things this way, you stay deluded and blind. For instance, when we chant, "*Jarā-dhammāmhi*—I am subject to death," that's simply to make us mindful and heedful in the beginning stages of the practice. When you reach the stage of insight meditation, though, there's none of that. All assumptions, all conventional truths get ripped away. They all collapse. When the body is empty of self, what is there to latch onto? Physical elements, mental elements, they're already empty of any self. You have to see this clearly, through and through. Otherwise, they gather together and form a being, both physical and mental, and then we latch onto them as being our self.

Once we see the world as elements, however, there's no death. And once we can see that there's no death, that's when we'll really *know.* If we still believe that *we* die, that shows that we haven't yet seen the Dhamma. We're still stuck on the outer shell. And when this is the case, what sort of Dhamma can we expect to know? You have to penetrate deeper in; you have to contemplate, take things apart.

You're almost at the end of your lease in this burning house, yet you continue latching onto it as your self. It tricks you into feeling fear and love, but if you fall for it, what path will you practice? The mind latches onto these things to fool itself on many, many levels. If you can't see through such conventions as "woman" or "man," you'll grasp hold of them as your self—and then you turn yourself into these things. If you can't empty yourself of these conventions and assumptions, your practice simply circles around in the same old place.

So you have to contemplate down through many levels. It's like using a cloth to filter things. If you use a coarse weave, you won't catch much of anything. You have to use a fine weave to filter out the small things—to move down to the deeper levels and penetrate *into* them, level after level. That's why there are many levels to being mindful and discerning, filtering down to the details.

And this is why becoming fully aware of your own inner character is so important. The practice of meditation is nothing but catching sight of self-deceptions, to see how they infiltrate into the deepest levels and how even the most blatant levels fool us right before our very eyes. If you can't catch sight of the deceits and deceptions of the self, your practice won't lead to release from suffering. It will simply keep you deluded into thinking that everything is you and yours.

To practice in line with the Buddha's teachings is to go *against* the flow. Every living being, deep down inside, wants pleasure on the physical level and then on the higher and more subtle levels of feeling, such as the types of concentration that are addicted to feelings of peace and respite. This is why you have to investigate into feeling so that you can let go of it and thus snuff out craving, through being fully aware of feeling as it actually is—free from any self—in line with its nature: unentangled, uninvolved. This is what snuffs out the virus of craving so that ultimately it vanishes without trace.

THE INTRICACIES OF IGNORANCE

There are many layers to self-deception. The more you practice and investigate, the less you feel like claiming to know. Instead, you'll simply see the harm of your own multifaceted ignorance and foolishness. Your examination of the viruses in the mind gets more and more subtle. When you don't know but think you do, you take your views to be knowledge. But actually the things you know aren't real knowledge. They're the understanding that comes from labels. Still, you think they're knowledge and you think *you* know. This in itself is a very intricate self-deception.

So we have to keep watch on these things, to keep contemplating them. Sometimes they fool us right before our eyes: That's when it really gets bad, because we don't know that we've got ourselves fooled, and instead think we're people who know. We may be able to deal thoroughly with this or that topic, but our knowledge is simply the memory of labels. We think that labels are discernment, or thought-fabrications are discernment, or the awareness of sensory consciousness is discernment, and so we get these things all mixed up. As a result, we become enamored with all the bits of knowledge that slip in and fashion the mind—which are simply the illusions within awareness. As for genuine awareness, there's very little of it, while deceptive awareness has us surrounded on all sides.

We thus have to contemplate and investigate until we see through these illusions in awareness. This is what will enable us to read the mind. If your awareness goes out, don't follow it out. Stop and turn inward instead. Whatever slips in to fashion the mind, you have to be wise to it. You can't forbid it, for it's something natural, and you shouldn't try to close off the mind too much. Simply keep watch on awareness to see how far it will go, how true or false it is, how it disbands and then arises again. Watch it over and over. By simply watching like this, you will be able to read yourself, to know cause and effect within yourself, and to contemplate yourself. This will make your mindfulness and discernment more skillful. If you don't practice in this way, the mind will remain dark. It may get a little empty, a little still, and then you'll decide that's plenty good enough.

But if you look at the Buddha's teachings, you'll find that no matter what sort of correct knowledge he gained, he was never willing to stop there. He always said, "There's more." To begin with, he developed mindfulness and alertness in every activity, but then he said, "There's more to do, further to go." As for us, we're always ready to brag. We work at developing this or that factor for a while and then say we know all about it and don't have to develop it further. As a result, the principles in our awareness go soft *because of our boastfulness and pride.*

EMPTINESS VERSUS THE VOID

Opening the door and really seeing inside yourself isn't easy, but you can train yourself to do it. If you have enough mindfulness to read yourself and understand yourself, that cuts through a lot of issues right there. Craving will have a hard time forming. In whatever guise it arises, you'll get to read it, to know it, to extinguish it, to let it go.

When you get to do these things, it doesn't mean that you "get" anything, for actually once the mind is empty, it doesn't gain anything at all. But to put it into words for those who haven't experienced it: In what ways is emptiness empty? Does it mean that everything disappears or is annihilated? Actually, emptiness doesn't mean that the mind is annihilated. All that's annihilated is clinging and attachment. What you have to do is this: See what emptiness is like as it actually appears and then not latch onto it. The nature of this emptiness is that it's deathless within you—this emptiness of self—and yet the mind can still function, know, and read itself. Just don't label it or latch onto it, that's all.

There are many levels of emptiness, many types, but if it's emptiness of this or that type, then it's not genuine emptiness, for it contains the intention that's trying to know what type of emptiness it is, what features it has. This is something you have to look into deeply if you really want to know. If it's superficial emptiness—the emptiness of the still mind, free from thought-fabrications about its objects or free from the external sense of self—that's not genuine emptiness. Genuine emptiness lies deep, not on the level of mere stillness or concentration. The emptiness of the void is something very profound.

But because of what we've studied and heard, we tend to label the emptiness of the still mind as the void—but this is labeling things wrongly in that emptiness. Actually it's just ordinary still-ness. We have to look more deeply. No matter what you've encountered or heard about before, don't get excited. Don't label it as this or that level of attainment. Otherwise you'll spoil everything. You reach the level where you should be able to keep your aware-ness steady, but once you label things, it stops right there—or else goes all out of control.

This labeling is attachment in action. It's very subtle, very refined. Whatever appears, it latches on. So you simply have to let the mind be empty without labeling it as anything. The emptiness that lets go of preoccupations or that's free from the influence of thought-fabrications *is something you have to look further into.* Don't label it as this or that level, for to measure and compare things in this way blocks everything—and in particular, knowledge of how the mind changes.

So to start out, simply watch these things, simply be aware. If you get excited, you'll ruin everything. Instead of seeing things clear through, you won't. You'll stop there and won't go any further. For this reason, when you train the mind or contemplate the mind to the point of gaining clear realizations every now and then, regard them as simply things to observe.

OPENING THE WAY IN THE HEART

Once you can read your mind correctly, you can catch hold of defile-ments and kill them off—that's insight meditation. The mind becomes razor sharp, just as if you have a sharp knife that can cut any-thing clear through. Even if defilements arise again, you can dig them up again, cut them off again. It's actually a lot of fun, this job of uprooting the defilements in the mind. There's no other work nearly as much fun as getting this sense of "I" or self under your thumb, because you get to see all of its tricks. It's really fun. Whenever it shows its face in order to get anything, you just watch it—to see what it wants and why it wants it, to see what inflated claims it makes for itself. This way you can cross-examine it and get to the facts.

Once you know, there's nothing to do but let go, to become unentangled and free. Just think of how good that can be! This practice of ours is a way of stopping and preventing all kinds of things inside ourselves. Whenever defilement rises up to get anything, to grab hold of anything, we don't play along. We disengage. Just this is enough to do away with a lot of stress and suffering, even though the defilements feel the heat.

When we oppress the defilements a lot, it gets them hot and feverish, you know. But remember, it's the *defilements* that get hot and feverish. And remember that the Buddha told us to put the heat on the defilements, because if we don't put the heat on them, they put the heat on us all the time.

So we must be intent on burning the defilements away, even though they may complain that we're mistreating them. We close the door and imprison them. Since they can't go anywhere, they're sure to complain: "I can't take it! I'm not free to go anywhere at all!" So simply watch them. Where do they want to go? What do they want to grab hold of? Watch them carefully, and they'll stop— stop going, stop running. It's easy to say no to other things, but saying no to yourself, saying no to your defilements, isn't easy at all—and yet it doesn't lie beyond your discernment or capabilities to do it. If you have the mindfulness and discernment to say no to defilement, it'll stop. Don't think that you can't make it stop. You *can*—it's simply that you've foolishly given in too quickly, and that's become second nature.

So we must stop. Once we stop, the defilements stop. Wherever they turn up, we can extinguish them. And when this is the case, how can we *not* want to practice? No matter how stubbornly they want anything, simply watch them. Get acquainted with them, and they won't stay. They'll disband. As soon as they disband, you realize exactly how deceptive they are. Before, you didn't know. When they urged you to do something, you went along. But once you're wise to them, they stop. They disband. Even though you don't disband them, they disband on their own. And as soon as you see their disbanding, the path opens wide before you. Everything opens wide in the heart. You can see that there's a way you can overcome defilement, you can put an end to defilement, no matter how much it arises. But you've got to remember to keep on watching out for it, keep on letting it go.

Thus I ask that you always make the effort to keep sharpening your tools. Once your discernment is sharp on any point, it can let go of that point and uproot it. If you look after that state of mind and contemplate how to keep it going, you'll be able to keep your tools from getting dull.

And now that you know the basic principles, I ask that you make the effort to the utmost of your strength and mindfulness. May you be brave and resilient, so that your practice for gaining release from suffering and stress reaps good results in every way.

PURE AND SIMPLE

In June 1973, the Khao Suan Luang community celebrated Upāsikā Kee's seventy-second birthday—an important milestone in a culture that calculates years in twelve-year cycles—by printing a collection of excerpts from her Dhamma talks. The following selections are drawn from that collection.

The first requirement when you come to practice is that you need to be the sort of person who loves the truth—and you need to possess endurance to do what's true. Only then will your practice get anywhere. Otherwise, it all turns into failure and you go back to being a slave to your defilements and cravings just as before.

When you don't contemplate yourself, how much suffering do you cause for yourself? And how much do you cause for others? These are things we should contemplate as much as we can. If we don't, we keep trying to get, get, get. We don't try to let go, to put things aside, to make any sacrifices at all. We just keep trying to get, for the more we get, the more we want.

If you're greedy and stingy, then even if you have loads of money the Buddha says you're poor: poor in noble treasures, poor in the treasures of the mind. Even if you have lots of external wealth, when you die it all goes to other people, it turns into common property, but you yourself are left poor in virtue, poor in the Dhamma.

A mind without its own home—a mind without the Dhamma as its home—has to live with the defilements. One defilement arises, and the mind goes running after it. As soon as it disappears, another arises over there, and the mind goes running after that one. Because the mind has no dwelling of its own, it runs wild all over the place.

Practicing to put an end to defilement and suffering is a high level of practice, so you first have to clear the ground and put it in good order. Don't think that you can practice without any preparation. If you live for your appetites, all you can think of is getting things to quench your appetites. If you don't develop a sense of contentment or a sense of shame on the beginning level, it'll be hard to practice the higher levels.

The important part of the practice lies in contemplating. If you don't contemplate, discernment won't arise. The Buddha taught us to contemplate and test things to the point where we can clearly know for ourselves. Only then will we have a proper refuge. He never taught us to take refuge in things we ourselves can't see or do.

If you truly want to gain release from suffering, you have to practice truly, you have to make a true effort. You have to let go, starting with outer things and working inward. You have to free yourself from the delusion that falls for alluring delights.

The important point in letting go is to see the drawbacks in whatever you're letting go of. Only then can you let it go once and for all. If you don't see its drawbacks, you'll still be attached and will miss having it around.

If you're going to let go of anything, you first have to see its drawbacks. If you just tell yourself, "Let go, let go," the mind won't easily obey. You really have to see the drawbacks in the thing you're holding on to, and then the mind will let go of its own accord. It's like grabbing hold of fire. When you feel the heat, you let go of your own accord and will never grasp it again.

❧

It's hard to see the drawbacks of sensual passion, but even harder to see the drawbacks of more subtle things, like your sense of self.

❧

On the beginning level of the practice you have to learn how to control your words and deeds—the level of virtue—so that you can keep your words and deeds at normalcy, calm and restrained. In this way, the mind won't follow the power of the crude defilements. When violent urges arise, first stop them with your power of endurance. After you've been able to endure for a while, your insight will gain the strength it needs to develop a sense of right and wrong, and in this way you'll see the worth of endurance, that it really is a good thing.

❧

When you do good, let it be good in line with nature. Don't latch onto the thought that *you're* good. If you get attached to the idea that you're good, it will give rise to lots of other attachments.

❧

When a mind without pride or conceit gets a scolding, it shrinks back like an ox hit by a stick. Your sense of self will disappear right before your eyes. A good ox, even it sees only the shadow of the whip or the stick, stays still and composed, ready to do quickly what it's told. A meditator who can reduce her pride and conceit is sure to make progress and will have nothing heavy to weigh down her mind. The mind will be still and empty—free from any attachment to "me" or "mine." This is how the mind grows empty.

If you're the sort of person who's open and honest, you'll find your window for disbanding suffering and defilement *right where you're honest with yourself, right where you come to your senses.* You don't have to go explaining high-level Dhamma to anyone. All you need is the ordinary level of being honest with yourself about the sufferings and drawbacks of your actions, so that you can put a stop to them, so that you develop a sense of wariness, a sense of shame. That's much better than talking about high-level Dhamma but then being heedless, complacent, and shameless.

When you look back, you see all your own heedlessness. Even though you knew the Buddha's teachings and were able to explain them correctly, still the heart and mind were heedless. Actually, people who know a lot of Dhamma and show off their knowledge can be more heedless than people who know only a little. Those who've never read Dhamma books tend to be more heedful, for they're more modest and know that they need to read their own minds. Those who've read a lot of books or heard a lot of talks tend to get complacent. And in this way they become heedless and disrespectful of the Dhamma.

✂

We have to figure out how to use our own mindfulness and discernment to look inward at all times, for no one else can know these things or see these things for us. We have to know for ourselves.

✂

When things are weak and watery, they flow away. When they're solid they don't flow. When the mind is weak and devoid of strength, it's always ready to flow away like water. But when the mind is endowed with mindfulness and discernment, when it's solid and true in its effort, it can withstand the flow of the defilements.

✂

When you first start meditating, it's like catching a monkey and tying it to a leash. When it's first tied down, it'll struggle with all its might to get away. In the same way, when the mind is first tied down to its meditation object, it doesn't like it. It'll struggle more than it normally would, which makes us feel weak and discouraged. So in this first stage we simply have to use our endurance to resist the mind's tendency to stray off in search of other objects. Over time it will gradually grow tame.

✂

You want the mind to be quiet but it won't be quiet. So what do you do, what do you focus on, what do you know, in order to see how the arising and passing away of fabrication occur? Try to look carefully and you're sure to know for yourself, for it's nothing hidden or mysterious. It's something whose basic principles you can see for yourself.

What can we do so that the mind doesn't get distracted with its preoccupations or its nonsensical mental fabrications? We have to give the mind something to focus its awareness on, for if its awareness isn't focused on one thing, it wanders around to know other things, other matters. This is why we practice focusing our awareness on the body, or on the breath, making the breath the post to which we tie our monkey—the mind. In other words, we use mindfulness to keep the mind focused on the breath. This is the first step in the practice.

Training the mind to stay focused on the breath is something we have to do continuously, with each in-and-out breath, in every posture—sitting, standing, walking, lying down. No matter what you're doing, stay focused on the breath. If you want, you can simply stay focused on nothing more than the sensation of the breath, without determining whether it's long or short. Keep breathing normally. Don't force the breath or hold the breath or sit with your body too tense. Sit straight and face comfortably straight ahead. If you're going to turn to the left, make sure to be focused on the breath as you turn. If you turn to the right, stay focused on the breath as you turn.

Whatever posture you use is up to you, but stay focused on the breath continuously. If your attention lapses, bring it back to knowing the breath again. Whatever you're doing at any time, watch the breath with every in-and-out breath and you'll be developing mindfulness and alertness—full-body self-awareness—at the same time you're being aware of the breath.

When you walk, you don't have to focus on the steps of the feet. Focus on the breath and let the feet do the stepping on their own. Let each part of the body perform its function on its own. All you have to do is stay focused on the breath and you'll have full-body awareness.

Whether the eye is looking at sights or the ear is listening to sounds, stay focused on the breath. When you look at a sight, make sure that knowing the breath underlies the looking. When you listen to a sound, make sure that knowing the breath underlies the listening. The breath is a means for making the mind quiet, so you first have to train yourself with it. Don't be in a hurry to get higher results. Train the mind to stay under the control of mindfulness continuously for days on end—to the point where the mind doesn't let its attention lapse. It will come to stay more and more with the breath, focused on knowing the breath continuously, and then other things will stop on their own: Thinking stops, speaking stops. Whatever tasks you have to do, you can still do them while at the same time keeping track of the breath each and every moment. If there are any lapses, you come back to knowing the breath again. There's nothing else you have to think about. Be aware of the breath at the same time you're aware of the normalcy of the mind.

When the mind can maintain its stance in normalcy, you can observe the breath and see that it's at normalcy, too. When their normalcy is in balance, you focus on knowing that the breath is simply a natural phenomenon—the wind element. The body as a whole is composed of the four elements: earth, water, fire, and wind. So here we're focused on the wind element. The wind element is a natural phenomenon, not us or ours. The mind is then at normalcy, not thinking or fabricating anything, not stirring things up. It, too, is a natural phenomenon, pure and simple. If it's not fabricated into anything else, if it's not burned by defilements, it can stay still and at normalcy.

When you stay focused on the breath in every posture, it's a means of blocking the mind from traipsing around with its thoughts and labels. You have to be intent on training the mind to stay with the breath with every posture: That's how you'll come to know what the mind is like when it has mindfulness of breathing as its dwelling place.

Focusing on the breath helps the mind grow quiet more than any other method—and it's not at all tiring. Simply breathe comfortably. If you let the breath come in and out strongly, it helps the breath energy and blood flow throughout the body. If you breathe deeply so that the stomach muscles relax, it helps to prevent constipation.

When you train with the breath, it exercises both the body and the mind, and in this way everything calms down in a natural way more easily than if we try to calm things down with force or threats. No matter how much you threaten the mind, it won't surrender. It'll run all over the place. So instead we train it to fall in line with nature—for after all, the breath is an aspect of nature. Whether you're aware of it or not, the breath breathes in line with its nature. Only when we focus on it are we aware of it. The body is also an aspect of nature. The mind is an aspect of nature. When they're trained in an appropriate way, there aren't a lot of problems that you have to solve. The flow of blood and breath energy in the body improves the state of your nerves. If you train your mindfulness and alertness to be aware of the whole body, and at the same time you're aware of the breath, the breath will flow effortlessly.

If you sit for long periods of time, this practice will help keep the blood and breath energy flowing naturally. You don't have to fight the breath or hold it in. When you place your feet and hands in the meditation posture, don't tense them up. If you relax them so that the blood and breath energy flow easily, it will be very helpful.

Focusing on mindfulness of the breath is appropriate in every way—appropriate for the body, appropriate for the mind. Before his Awakening, when he was still a bodhisattva, the Buddha used mindfulness of breathing more than any other practice as the dwelling place for his mind. So when you practice it, you too will have mindfulness of breathing as the dwelling place for your mind. That way the mind won't wander around fabricating thoughts and getting embroiled. You have to get it to settle down and be still. As soon as anything springs up, focus on the breath. If you try to focus directly on the mind right from the start, it might be too difficult to manage if you're not familiar with it.

If you want to focus directly on the mind, that's fine, too, but you have to be aware of it with every in-and-out breath. Make your awareness continuous for long periods of time.

Work at this in every posture and see what results arise. In the beginning you have to put together the causes—in other words, you have to make an effort to look and know *correctly*. As for the letting go, that comes afterward.

The Buddha compared the training of the mind to holding a bird in your hand. The mind is like a tiny bird, and the question is how to hold the bird so that it doesn't fly away. If you hold it too tightly, it will die in your hand. If you hold it too loosely, the tiny bird will slip out through your fingers. So how are you going to hold it so that it doesn't die and doesn't get away? The same holds true with our training of the mind in a way that's not too tense and not too lax but always just right.

There are many things you have to know in training the mind, and you have to look after them correctly. On the physical side, you have to change postures in a way that's balanced and just right so that the mind can stay at normalcy, so that it can stay at a natural level of stillness or emptiness continuously.

Physical exercise is also necessary. Even yogis who practice high levels of concentration have to exercise the body by stretching and bending it in various postures. We don't have to go to extremes like them, but we can exercise enough so that the mind can maintain its stillness naturally, in a way that allows it to contemplate physical and mental phenomena and see them as inconstant, stressful, and not-self.

If you force the mind too much, it dies just like the bird held too tightly. In other words, it grows deadened, insensitive, and will simply stay frozen in stillness without contemplating to see what inconstancy, stress, and not-selfness are like.

Our practice is to make the mind still enough so that it can contemplate inconstancy, stress, and not-selfness. This is the point for which we train and contemplate, and that makes the training easy.

As for changing postures or working and getting exercise, we do these things with an empty mind.

When you're practicing in total seclusion, you should get some physical exercise. If you simply sit and lie down, the flow of blood and breath energy in the body will get abnormal.

The fourth tetrad in the instructions for keeping the breath in mind begins with keeping track of inconstancy with every in-and-out breath. Maintaining this kind of awareness for long is difficult because we don't maintain our awareness with every in-and-out breath. When things grow empty, we just let the mind grow quiet, without focusing or contemplating, so everything drifts or grows blurry. Or some sort of fabrication arises so we can't focus on the empty mind.

So when a crude fabrication arises, block it by focusing on the breath. Use the breath to snuff it out. Whether the fabrication is a tiny or a strong sensation, catch hold of the breath as your first step in protecting yourself. The more often you do this, the more it turns into a normal habit—and the more useful it will be.

Simply staying with the breath can help prevent unskillful thinking—in other words, it can keep the mind from fabricating unskillful thoughts. That way, craving for sights, sounds, smells, tastes, and tactile sensations can't take shape. Whatever you're aware of, quickly focus on the breath, and whatever it is, it will simply stop and disband.

When the mind is very refined and very still, if you don't maintain your focus, your awareness can blur or grow distracted. So you have to keep your mindfulness in focus. Breathe deeply and heavily as a way of waking the mind up. Don't let it grow quiet in an unfocused way.

You have to focus on seeing the condition of emptiness within the mind, which is a primal part of its nature. If you can do this, there's not much else to the practice. Simply keep the mind under the control of mindfulness and the breath. In other words, keep watching it, knowing it. Even if there's some thinking that helps in your knowing, *keep it short.* Don't let it grow long. Whatever the reflection or the contemplation, keep it short. Don't let it grow long. If it's long, it'll turn into distraction.

Use the breath as a means of cutting it off. When your thinking starts getting long, make it stop. Keep it as short as possible. Keep your self-awareness as still, clear, and bright as possible, and keep seeing that it doesn't have any self.

The mind that maintains itself in a state of normalcy is like a white cloth or a white sheet of paper. You have to keep focused on keeping watch over it to see, when there's any sensory contact, how the mind wavers in reaction, how it labels things as "good" or "bad" or "self." This is something you have to learn how to observe on a refined level.

Once the mind is quiet and empty, your awareness really gets sharper. "Sharp" here means that it sees the actual facts because it focuses its gaze and sees clearly. If you're looking at something and don't yet see clearly, don't go looking anywhere else. Keep looking right there until you know.

What does this knowing know? It knows arising, remaining, passing away. And it doesn't cling. To know in this way you have to keep abreast of fabrication of every sort, whether it fabricates good or bad or neither good nor bad.

If you're not yet capable of contemplating the mind, then contemplate the body to see how it's composed of the four elements: earth, water, wind, and fire. You have to keep eating and excreting, adding elements and excreting them all the time. Even just the affairs of the body—of this walking corpse—are already a burden. When it's hot you have to give it a shower; when it's cold you have to wrap it up in blankets; when it's sick you have to give it medicine; when it's hungry you have to give it food. You have to look after it in just the right way; otherwise it causes all sorts of problems.

They say that the mind is the master, and the body the servant. But if craving becomes the mind's master, then the body will have two masters. Just think of how many conflicts that can cause! The mind is in bad straits and so is the body.

The physical body on its own is already painful and stressful. If we fasten onto it, that makes it even more painful and stressful. So contemplate the body carefully. See that there's only the stress of conditions, the stress of the aggregates, but that there's no one to whom the stress belongs—and there's no defilement burning the heart.

Give up your fascination with worthless things, with the good and bad things of the past. Sweep them up and toss them out. Make the mind free of clutter. And once it's free of clutter, don't go gathering up things to clutter it up again. For example, your mind is empty at the moment. Look at it to see how things take shape and arise; look at how they disappear. Look at genuine nature right here. Look at the nature of how the mind receives its objects, or how it receives contact. If you see correctly in line with the truth, you'll see that these things are all empty. There's nothing true or lasting about them at all. Simply look in a way that doesn't apply labels. When the eye sees sights or the ear hears sounds, look at these things simply as natural events. As for the mind, let it stay still, free from any tendency to get involved by labeling things as good or bad. That way desire won't arise to disturb the mind.

Ask yourself: If you fall for these things and suffering follows, what do you get out of it? You'll see that you don't get anything at all. It's all empty. What you *do* get is the suffering that keeps the heart flustered. So whatever you look at, see its inconstancy thoroughly, inside and out. Just that will be enough to keep you from having to cling to anything.

When you're aware of sensory contact, you don't want your awareness to stop just at the point where the eye sees a sight or the ear hears a sound. You have to look deeply into the eye-consciousness that takes note of the sight. Then focus on the sensation of sight to see how it changes, how it decays and disbands.

If you understand how to look, you can see the changes in physical and mental phenomena of all kinds. Physical phenomena you can see with your eyes. For example, a flower that's still fresh contains change and decay right there in its freshness. If you see its decay only when it's withered and brown, your contemplation is still crude, still far from the truth.

Nothing that's fabricated is stable or steady, but we make up our own suppositions about these things. Things change in the direction of development and in the direction of decay. We see these as two separate processes, but actually both of them are decay.

Whenever there's sensory contact, keep your focus turned inward on the mind continuously. Keep it still and at normalcy. As for the contact, simply know it as contact, but keep your awareness of the mind as continuous as possible until all your awareness gathers together. Let it gather into an awareness pure and simple. If this pure and simple awareness can maintain its stance continuously, it will become a means of reading and deciphering everything within. You don't have to pay attention to the sensations of arising and passing away. Focus instead on the awareness pure and simple—in other words, the awareness right at the mind or at the property of consciousness pure and simple. Even if you're aware of physical matters, keep your awareness pure and simple.

You have to be observant when the mind has firmly established mindfulness and your awareness gathers so that you're aware of the property of consciousness, pure and simple, without any fabrication at all—an awareness pure and simple right at itself. Take that as your foundation.

In the beginning we focus on the breath to keep the mind from wandering off. When you focus on the breath as it grows more and more refined, you get to the point where you don't have to focus on the breath any more. You focus continually right at the mind. You focus right on the mind pure and simple, without any fabrications, without any labels. Whatever arises, know it no further than that and keep your mindfulness continuous.

When the mind lies under the control of mindfulness, without fabricating thoughts or getting distracted, it will be quiet and awake within. When you focus directly on the mind, it will stop and grow still naturally. You'll see that the mind is just an aspect of nature, not your "self" or anything of the sort. When you see clearly that it's just an aspect of nature, that will destroy any attachment to it as "you" or "yours."

Whether you're aware of forms or feelings, simply let them be aspects of nature—all of them. The mind won't be put to difficulties, won't get stirred up with thoughts and fabrications. Let it stop and grow still, simply by keeping abreast of itself with every moment.

※

To restrain the mind makes the sensations of sensory contact stop in their tracks. In other words, simply being acquainted with the mind when mindfulness is focused on being aware of the mind allows sensory contacts to pass away naturally right in the present. This is why people who are careless, who don't develop restraint through mindfulness, fall easily under the power of the defilements.

Restraint through mindfulness is the first step. You maintain restraint by being mindful. When your mindfulness becomes continuous to the point where it becomes clear knowing, that's called restraint through knowledge. Try to maintain this state of clear knowing within.

※

Restraint of the senses is for the purpose of seeing the movements of the mind—to see how the sensation of contact at the eye, ear, nose, tongue, body, or mind turns into other sensations.

※

Your study of the Dhamma has to be a study inside, not a study of written words or spoken words. It has to be a study of the mind pure and simple so that it will know its own features and characteristics while it maintains its normalcy or maintains itself in emptiness, an emptiness that doesn't latch onto anything.

If you look at it again and again with every moment, it will develop into a clear awareness of the characteristics of an aspect of nature fabricated from causes and conditions, simply on the level of its own nature, pure and simple. Or there may be an awareness of another side of nature—even though the awareness may not be clear—of an aspect of nature free from fabrication. Here I'm referring to the mind that's empty or quiet on its own, which can serve as a standard for comparison. The aspect of the mind fabricated by conditions is simply nature. Don't enter into it to latch onto it. As for the aspect that's not fabricated, that's simply empty in and of itself: This too shouldn't be latched onto.

So if, when the mind is embroiled, you latch onto the idea that "my mind is embroiled"—or if, when the mind is empty, you latch onto the idea that "my mind is empty"—see that both of these are equal, in that no matter what you latch onto, you have to suffer. So no matter how things change, if you correctly know the truth of the Buddha's *sabbe dhammā anattā*—all phenomena are not-self—you'll simply be able to let go.

Stopping to look, stopping to know your own mind, is better than straying out to know things outside, for when you stop to look, stop to know, you'll see inconstancy, stress, and not-selfness in a way that doesn't require words. This will be a knowing that's totally silent and still within. *The kind of insight that uses the words "inconstant," "stressful," and "not-self" is imitation knowing, not the real thing.* Genuine knowing sees the change happening with every moment right before your eyes, right here and now. You actually see whatever arises and how it passes away. And it's always there for you to see right now.

There's nothing difficult about it at all. So if you know how to stop to look, stop to know your own mind, you'll become acquainted with the Dhamma in a correct way.

If you look correctly, seeing all the way through, you'll see how change involves arising, remaining, and passing away with every moment. You'll see how change inherently involves stress. But you have to see all the way in, in a profound way. It's not just a matter of repeating to yourself that these things are inconstant, stressful, and not-self.

You really have to look in order to see how change is inherently stressful. You don't have to call it "stressful" in your mind, but you have to see this truth clearly right in the stress itself. Once you've seen that inconstancy is stressful, you'll see the non-selfness inherently there in the same place.

If you stay focused on disbanding this, that, and the other thing, you've fallen for the deceits of inconstancy.

When you look at inconstancy, or arising and passing away, with true mindfulness and discernment, there will have to be a sense of dismay, disenchantment, and dispassion. If you know but are simply indifferent, that's called not knowing. You've simply fooled yourself into thinking you know when you really don't. Genuine knowing, bright and clear to the heart, is something else entirely—not at all the indifferent knowing that counts as delusion.

When you really know, there has to be a sense of dismay, a sense of urgency in getting everything out, giving everything back, a sense of urgency in seeing how things are not at all worthy of attachment. That's the kind of knowing you have to develop. If you haven't yet developed it, you need to contemplate things over and over, whether you're sitting, standing, walking, lying down, eating, excreting, or whatever. You need to be absorbed in contemplating these things as much as you can. When you can do that, you'll enter into the Dhamma. If the mind is still far away and distracted, if it's still concerned with this, that, and the other thing, it'll keep retreating further and further away until it falls slave to craving and defilement as before.

The chant for contemplating the four requisites is very useful and beneficial. You have to keep training yourself not to get carried away in your consumption of the requisites. The mindfulness that arises from this contemplation will then be full of discernment. Wherever there's mindfulness, there has to be alertness and self-awareness—which are the same thing as discernment.

Every aspect of the training that aims at making you contented with what you have helps keep the mind more empty than not. Once you see the value of these practices, you should practice letting go of your desires. If you simply follow your desires, then if you get what you desire you're happy. If you don't, you get all hot and bothered. So contemplate desire to see if it's stressful—to see how it's both stress and the cause of stress all in one.

Training the mind is refined work. Even when knowledge arises, if you decide on your own that it's right for sure, you've failed the test. No matter what the knowledge, if it can waver, it's fake knowledge, deceptive knowledge, not absolute knowledge.

When you latch onto your knowledge as correct, that gives rise to wrong view *in that very moment.* So you have to keep stopping, looking, and knowing until you see how your knowing turns into not-knowing. This is because right knowing and wrong knowing are inherently intertwined. It's not the case that true knowing will stay as nothing but true knowing. You have to find the angle from which you can see how and where wrong knowing and wrong views will spring up.

When pride and conceit arise, you have to make them turn around and contemplate themselves, to see that there's no "self" to them— and so when that's the case, what do they get out of bragging? Exactly where is their self? When you look into this, you find that you're at a loss as to what to say. And that in itself helps to put an end to your bragging.

When you find the source that gives rise to "I know, I'm right, I'm good," that's the voice you have to make life difficult for. If you make life difficult for other voices in the mind, you've missed the mark, for they're all just its followers.

The voice that says it's good or right: Use that voice to take itself apart. You don't have to use any other voice. Make it turn around and dig up its own source.

If you don't know how to look for your own faults, you're not practicing the Dhamma. To focus on your own faults goes against the flow. The basic principle in contemplation is that you can't put yourself first. You have to put the Dhamma first.

The more you know, the more modest you become: That's the nature of the Dhamma. Whoever says you're stupid, let them go ahead and say it, but make sure you stay full of the Dhamma inside. Maintain the Dhamma at all costs, in the same way that people carefully protect a cabinet in which the scriptures are kept. Focus on gathering the Dhamma into one point, keeping the mind in a proper stance without fastening onto anything. And as to how you protect it, and how it requires care and circumspection, that's something you have to discover for yourself.

Right views and right awareness see everything as Dhamma. In other words, they see all the events of fabrication in line with the three characteristics.

We have to contemplate the genuine essence of the Dhamma so that when we look outward we can see it all as Dhamma, without labeling it as good or bad. Try using your eyes to look in a way that doesn't involve labeling. See everything as nature following in line with causes and conditions. Or see everything as Dhamma pure and simple. Then see if the mind feels open, empty, and light.

The Dhamma that you can study in books is not the genuine essence of the Dhamma. To see the genuine essence of the Dhamma you have to strip away all conventional formulations, leaving nature pure and simple, free of any "being" or "having."

Contemplation that uses thoughts is still external. Internal contemplation has to be a focused watching that's motionless and still. It's a contemplation composed of focused watching, not something thought out.

Your contemplation has to go through many layers, not just one. The first layer is to watch on the level of perceptions and labels. Next you watch thoughts. And then next you watch awareness.

If you're watching labels, see them simply as labels: the act of recognition, the awareness that you've recognized something. Then the label disbands.

If you're watching thoughts, see how a thought arises, see what it's about, and then see how it disbands. Then a new thought arises, and it too disbands. This is the second level.

Then you watch awareness, the awareness of the mind pure and simple, a sensation that arises right at the mind. Watch that sensation right at the mind and see how it disbands in just the same way.

We have to use mindfulness and discernment, which are like extremely sharp shovels and hoes, to dig down to our sense of self. Then we can turn it over and look at it from all sides to see exactly where it's our self. Try contemplating the form, feeling, perception, fabrication, or consciousness that you hold on to so tightly, to see exactly where it's constant, pleasurable, or self.

We haven't contemplated the pile of five aggregates—which is changing before our very eyes—in order to see correctly its natural conditions as they appear. That's why we've fallen for the allure of attachment and clinging that give rise to the sense of self that functions as the "taker," the "consumer," the "receiver of results." And then we have to suffer by entering into the consuming and receiving—all without realizing it. In fact, we want more. For instance, when we receive the results of a mind that's quiet and at ease, we want them to stay that way. When they change, we get all stirred up. But if we understand the principles of inconstancy, stress, and not-self, we can let go. We don't have to hold on tight. Right here is the path to release.

You've come here to practice specifically to put an end to your suffering and defilements, so you have to forget everything else. You don't have to concern yourself with lots of things. Simply focus your attention on your own body and mind, and everything will grow empty on its own. You don't have to go desiring the emptiness. Don't get yourself embroiled because of desire.

Instead of letting go of the things you should let go of, you feed them more fuel so that they flare up even stronger. Instead of dealing with the things you should abstain from or give up or weaken or destroy, you don't deal with them at all. And then you keep looking for new meditation techniques! Your defilements are arising right in your face, right in the mind, with every moment, and yet you don't deal with them. All you do is look for things outside to deceive yourself.

The practice of the Dhamma is a way of curing the illnesses inside the heart and mind, so we have to devote ourselves to the practice to the utmost of our abilities. We have to practice heedfully so that defilement, craving, and clinging will grow lighter. We have to focus and contemplate continuously at all times so as to destroy our attachment to self. This is the most important work in our lives: contemplating physical and mental phenomena to see their inconstancy, stress, and not-selfness. And we have to keep at this work throughout life as long as the defilements haven't yet ended. We keep looking, contemplating, letting go continually.

The hot defilements are easy to see, but the cool, damp defilements—such as love, desire, affection—that burn the mind with a cool, damp fire and are as poisonous as acid, these are harder to see. You have to examine yourself so that you know them for what they are. Otherwise you'll keep accumulating the fungus that causes damp rot within you.

The more your attention goes leaking outside, the more stupid you become. The more you focus inside, the sharper you become—and the more you'll be able to disband your suffering and defilements. The more you focus outside, the more you pick up the fungus that causes damp rot, and the more you become a garbage pit.

When we see defilements showing themselves in other people, we see how ugly they are. But when they show up in ourselves, we see them as good and right. This is where we're inconsistent, seeing our own defilements as our close friends—in line with the motto "Seeing a bladed discus as a petaled lotus." Is that the way we are? This is something really worth looking into.

If you know how to focus on the arising of defilement—whether it's greed or anger—even if it arises only a little bit, you should focus on staring it down to the point where you can snuff it out. If you don't make use of this approach, you won't have the strength to fight it off. If you feed it fuel until it starts fabricating all out of bounds, it will flare up as a huge fire and you won't be able to put it out. If you want to put it out, you have to snuff it out in the very first stage, when it appears as a slight sense of liking or disliking.

When the mind is empty, as it is now, keep contemplating how these feelings arise. See how they disappear and how you can make sure that nothing else will arise to fabricate them. Your awareness of the stem-point of fabrication is a means of snuffing out suffering right from the start—a means that's correct and uses the least strength.

Snuffing out blatant greed and anger isn't easy, for their roots are still in place; they're still nourished by fertilizer. That's why they keep flowering and bearing fruit. So if we really want to take the approach that's quickest and most correct, we have to focus on destroying delusion—on familiarizing ourselves with the truth.

Focus right on the issue of how defilements make the mind murky, bothered, and hot. Then contemplate how to disband them. When they disband, does the mind feel cool? Keep looking right there.

The coolness here doesn't come from our making it cool. It's cool in and of itself, without our having to shower it with water. It's the feeling-tone of the mind when it can let go of something. It's cool in and of itself.

Contemplating yourself repeatedly gives you a sense of the mind's higher nature that can pull you to release. It's a means of dispersing the habit of the mind that fastens onto things and leads the mind to grow ever weaker. Release comes through the power of mindfulness and discernment, not through the power of defilement, craving, or clinging.

When the mind is struggling to get something, just watch it at first. Only when it stops struggling should you deal with the issue in line with what's appropriate. In this way, desire will grow weaker, and your actions will fall under the power of mindfulness and discernment.

If we don't experiment with using the power of mindfulness and discernment to win out over defilement, we'll stay ignorant. We'll just keep on eating and living at our own convenience, but when anything strikes we'll start spinning away, grasping after all kinds of things. This is because we haven't worked at developing endurance and tolerance. We haven't trained ourselves to endure looking at pain and suffering, to endure focusing on pain and suffering, to see how heavy they are, to see *whose* pain and suffering they are. Only if we endure focusing on the pain and suffering until they dissipate will we benefit greatly from our practice.

We have to train ourselves to contemplate pain, focusing on it to the point where the mind doesn't fall in line with it and can let go. The pain then doesn't go any further than the body. As for pleasure, you don't have to latch onto it. You don't have to be pleased by pleasure. You have to see pleasure and pain as equal. They're equally inconstant and stressful, as they've been from the very beginning.

No matter how pain arises while sitting in meditation, you have to endure looking at it until you can let it go. See it as the stress of physical and mental phenomena, or the stress of the aggregates. As for the mind, keep it in a state of normalcy, without struggling. In this way, craving won't arise. If you let craving arise, you'll have a hard time letting it go. It'll thrash all around.

Simply be involved in watching the pain. When it arises, let it arise. If it's strong, simply know that it's strong. Don't let craving arise. Let there just be the feeling in and of itself. Notice how it takes shape, how it changes, and simply watch it that way. Keep any craving at bay.

Or if you want, you can turn and look at the mind pure and simple. If it's in a turmoil, you can know that craving has already arisen. If it's at normalcy, watch over it carefully, for it can pick up moods very quickly. If your attention lapses, it'll go flowing along with a mood.

When you go chasing after good and bad, and latch onto your sense of self, you create a huge fuss. But when you really know clearly, you sort out these problems so that they fade away. When you really examine all the evidence, you'll see that there's no good or bad arising. It all disbands. But then new thought fabrications arise and pass away, arise and pass away. They keep on flowing, and they seem to involve many, many issues. But actually there aren't many issues. *There's only arising, remaining, and passing away.* It's because we're not focused on knowing this that there seem to be so many issues. But no matter how many there are, there's just this: arising, remaining, and passing away, one after another, like a rippling current of water, where the rippling isn't a thing at all.

If you look into the rippling current of your thoughts, fabricating good and bad, you'll find that there's nothing you can latch onto as having any essence, for all these thoughts disband and disappear. If you learn how to look skillfully in this way, your mind will be empty, for you'll see the truth that these things all arise, remain, and pass away. The past has passed away. The future hasn't yet come. Look simply at the present arising and passing away right before your eyes—and don't latch on.

When you see arising, remaining, and passing away, pure and simple, right in the present moment and then can let go, that's when you gain release.

There's an old saying:
A flagpole planted
in a swift-flowing stream:
Right there's the Buddha
whose Dhamma's supreme.

In a swift-flowing stream refers to the present, where there's fabrication, change, arising and passing away. *Right there's the Buddha whose Dhamma's supreme* means that clear knowing is found right there. Letting go of attachment occurs right there.

Examine your mind to see what kind of currents it's flowing after. Stop and look at them. Be aware of them. Ultimately, you'll see that there's actually nothing there, just arising and passing away in emptiness, like a projected image that flashes into being and disappears, empty of any essence.

If your looking inward sees all the way through, you'll see that none of the things of the world have any value at all, for the highest value lies with the mind imbued with clear knowing, bright and clean. Even if this knowing is only momentary, it means that your practice isn't in vain. You can take it as your guide. Continue following it until you disband suffering and defilement without trace.

The internal sense of the mind will show itself of its own accord. It's like a diamond embedded in rock: When the rock is cut away, the diamond sparkles and shines. In the same way, when the mind is embedded in defilement, craving, and clinging, it's totally dark, totally in the dark. There's no light or brightness to it at all. But when our cutting tools—mindfulness and discernment—expose its facets, the mind will shine bright on its own.

The Dhamma covers many topics, but they're all gathered at the mind. Defilements are a kind of dhamma, as are discernment and the five aggregates. Everything's dhamma. Now, what we want is the highest dhamma, the dhamma that's unfabricated. We want to know what it's like, so where does it lie? It lies right here in the mind. The mind that isn't fabricated, that's empty of itself: That's the genuine dhamma.

In contemplating the phenomena of the present—the way things arise, remain, and disband—you have to keep looking until you see through to that which doesn't arise or disband. When you fully comprehend arising, remaining, and disbanding, you'll come face to face with emptiness.

Emptiness isn't empty in the way you'd sit and say to yourself, "There's nothing there at all." There are things there. The eye sees sights, the ear hears sounds, and so on. They're empty simply in that the mind doesn't enter in to label them, to concoct anything out of them, to cling to them, to like or dislike them. They're empty in that the mind is free from attachment, that's all.

If you don't know how to extinguish things, how to let go, you'll get stuck on every level of the path. If you get stuck on the delicious flavor of emptiness or stillness, *that's delusion's version of nibbāna.*

The practice requires that you pass through a lot of things. If you gain new knowledge and latch onto it, that will create an obstacle along your way. It's like taking a journey. If you run across something strange and new, and you're not willing to continue along your way because you get contented with where you already are, you'll end up setting up house right there. Your ability to continue on the journey depends on an awareness that sees clearly all the way through. If you set up house right here, thinking that nibbāna lies right here at the emptiness, that blocks your way. But if you take that sense of stillness and emptiness simply as a resting spot, it holds little danger, for you still have the opportunity to continue along your way.

The path that snuffs out defilement has to focus on snuffing out the view that latches onto knowledge and views.

You have to recognize the stages of the path that you need as resting spots, and to realize that you're holding on to them simply as temporary dwellings. If you grip them tightly, you'll get stuck there and will go no further.

If your awareness focuses down like this again and again and again, the mind will ultimately have to surrender. Its old habit of wandering around to know this and that will gradually calm down and grow still without your having to force it, for it won't be able to withstand your constant gaze. Every time you look at it, you'll see its deceptiveness. You'll see that it's not worthy of credence, not worthy of attachment, and so its deceptiveness will shrink away.

It's like a person who comes to flatter you. As soon as you focus your gaze on him and realize what he's up to, he has to shrink away in embarrassment.

To focus on the point where your sense of self arises, your mindfulness and discernment have to develop many approaches from many angles, using tricks that you figure out on your own.

The basic trick is a small thing: *Look for the point where the sense of self disbands on its own.*

If your awareness doesn't penetrate clearly into the disbanding of the property of consciousness, there's no way you can know how mental states arise and pass away. There's no way you can know how they wander around to take on objects, how they fall into the swirling currents of good and bad thought-fabrication, or how they get all wound up in a turmoil. So when you choose your focus, focus directly on the disbanding of mental states. When they take on an object, do they then disband? Keep looking until you can see how they disband on their own. If you can't manage this, focus first on the disbanding of physical and mental phenomena. When you clearly see the disbanding of physical and mental phenomena, you'll know for yourself how the consciousness which knows that disbanding also disbands on its own, each and every moment it knows those things.

Knowing the disbanding of consciousness is very useful. No matter how it arises, consciousness always disbands on its own. When you see this, you won't latch onto the idea that it has a self of any kind.

To know the disbanding of consciousness pure and simple is to know the disbanding of everything. It's like opening up the entire world, or stripping off the entire world and throwing it away.

When you can strip it away, throw it off, and let it go, there's nothing but emptiness, an emptiness that's bright and clear, with no sense of the world at all. The words "world" and "five aggregates" are simply conventions to help us see how there's change.

To become acquainted with the property of awareness pure and simple, you have to observe the mind's movements in response to contact. You have to know the arising and passing away of things, and you have to observe the awareness that accompanies the mind, which lies deep within the mind or in the property of consciousness. If it's not fabricated or labeled, it will stay quiet. It will maintain its stance. If you want to see how long it can maintain its stance, you have to observe its movements in response to contact or in response to the internal sensation of labeling. When these things arise, can that awareness maintain its stance? If it can't, it will get fabricated into distraction. And by the time the matter calms down, you'll be worn out.

If you can see into the condition of awareness pure and simple, you'll know your foundation—your inner foundation. In the beginning, you have to depend on mindfulness as your foundation for focusing. Then you focus on knowing the condition of change, of arising and passing away. This is focused looking, not simple looking.

Simple looking doesn't lead to any knowledge. It's delusion. Focused looking, sustained to the point of giving rise to clear knowing, is, in and of itself, a means of destroying delusion. On whatever level you're free from fabrication, from mental labels, or free from attachment, it's a means of clear knowing within the mind or the property of consciousness.

For your awareness to reach into the gathering point of the mind or of the property of consciousness pure and simple, you have to focus on the condition of change within the mind itself. You do this to destroy the deep seeds in the property of consciousness. These seeds, which lie continually in the property of consciousness, are very refined.

These are the seeds of sensual craving, craving for becoming, and craving for nonbecoming. Sensual craving is fairly easy to observe. The way it moves in to create desire for sights, sounds, smells, tastes, and tactile sensations is something fairly easy to see. As for the more latent seeds of craving for becoming—the craving to be or have a self or things belonging to a self—these lie deep. So we have to look deep if we want to destroy them.

If you can see all the way through to these seeds and can destroy them, that will be your path to release from suffering. This gathering point of the property of consciousness pure and simple, or of the property of awareness pure and simple, is thus something really worth looking into. If you don't gather your awareness to look into this point, you'll find it hard to destroy the seeds. Whatever seeds you do destroy will be external seeds, such as those of sensory pleasures. But the seeds that are latent tendencies lying within the mind or the property of consciousness have no intentions of their own. That's why we rarely see all the way into them, why we rarely know them. This is because we play around with their children, their followers: sensory pleasures. We don't focus inside to get any perspective at all.

Unintentional tendencies lie deep in your character. You can't intentionally get rid of them at the drop of a hat. The only way to get rid of them is to contemplate inwardly step by step so that you know them clearly. *You have to reach the basic level of unintentional knowing if you want to get rid of the unintentional things in the mind.*

The property of consciousness contains within it the sense of being or having a self. It contains the seeds that give rise to *being* and *having* in the same way that a seed contains bark, branches, and leaves. If you focus on knowing the condition of the property of name and form pure and simple, that itself will destroy the seeds for rebirth.

We have to contemplate natural conditions of two sorts: the changing condition of such things as the aggregates, and the unchanging condition of the total disbanding of suffering.

The first sort keeps changing its disguises without respite, deceiving us into latching onto it as genuine and true. Our fascination with pleasurable feelings is particularly deceptive. Even when we train the mind to be still, we're hoping for the delicious flavor of the pleasurable feeling. This is because we haven't contemplated the deceptiveness of feelings of every sort.

Some arahants gain Awakening through becoming acquainted with feeling and destroying the obsessions that lie latent in the three kinds of feeling: painful, pleasant, and neither painful nor pleasant.

Obsession with irritation lies latent in painful feeling. As soon as pain arises, whether it's mental or physical pain, irritation arises in the mind.

Obsession with passion lies latent in pleasant feeling. We like pleasure of every kind, wanting it to stay with us for a long time.

When a feeling of equanimity—neither pleasure nor pain—arises, we get absorbed in the equanimity because we don't know that it's just a feeling that has to arise and pass away in line with its conditions. This is why obsession with ignorance lies latent in equanimous feeling.

How do we let go of these obsessions? This is something to which we should give a lot of attention, because feeling has a lot of allure that can engender craving.

For example, when the mind is still and empty and then changes so that it's no longer still and empty, we want it to be still and empty again. The more we want, the more it's not empty.

If we can disband the desire for emptiness, that will let the mind grow empty again. Desire is what gets the mind embroiled in a turmoil, so desire is what we have to disband.

We practice restraint of the senses so as to disband desire, because the mind is always desiring to see the sights, hear the sounds, smell the aromas, taste the flavors, and sense the tactile sensations surrounding it.

It's because we don't know how desire is the cause of suffering that we struggle to satisfy our desires—and then all kinds of suffering follow.

The word *saṅkhata-dhamma*—fabricated phenomena—covers conditions of nature that are marked by the three characteristics. The things we have to study are summarized in two words: *saṅkhata dhamma* and *asaṅkhata dhamma*. Both terms have a deep and wide range of meaning, especially *saṅkhata dhammas,* which are always inconstant, stressful, and not-self. The conditions of *saṅkhata dhammas* follow their own swirling currents without end. As for *asaṅkhata dhamma*—the phenomenon that doesn't change, isn't stressful, but is still not-self—that's hard to know. But even this refined, subtle condition is something that we shouldn't latch onto.

When the mind stops, grows still, and is aware of itself, let it focus even more deeply on itself, for its stopping state is the mental state that's concentrated or in equanimity: still, neutral, neither pleased nor displeased. This is a type of fabrication called *aneñjābhisaṅkhāra—*

imperturbable fabrication—or if you want, you can call it neutral fabrication. When you focus on it, see it simply as an aspect of nature. Don't get sucked into the stillness, the neutrality, or the equanimity. At the same time, though, you do have to depend on the equanimity to see things as aspects of nature, pure and simple. This is a way of disbanding any fabrication of liking or disliking, good or bad. For this reason, we don't stop just at the equanimity. We have to see all the way through it and recognize that it's an aspect of nature free of self.

When the fabricated aspects of nature disband, the mind stays with its awareness of equanimity. Then you focus on the equanimity, just being aware of it as an aspect of nature, without using any labels or words. Simply focus on it, watch it, and become acquainted with the aspect of nature that lies further in, without labeling anything at all.

As you see into every level of nature pure and simple, things get deeper and more profound. You know and let go, know and let go, know and let go—*empty!*

Whatever appears, you let go. The important principle in your gazing inward is simply to let go.

You look, you see, and you let go. Incline the mind to letting go. Look in absolute stillness, with no inner conversation. Know and let go. Mindfulness keeps knowing through letting go of everything. The breath doesn't disappear. No matter how still or empty the mind, you're aware with every breath. If you don't know in this way, you'll soon lose focus and get distracted, or a fabrication of some sort will interfere so that you lose your foundation.

When the mind fabricates unskillful thoughts—thoughts of sensual passion, thoughts of ill will, thoughts of harmfulness—these are all called demeritorious fabrications *(apuññābhisaṅkhāra)*.

When the mind gains a sense of the drawbacks of sensual passion and develops a sense of distrust, disgust, and distaste for sensual passion, that's how you cleanse the mind so that it's not stuck on sensual passion, so that it's stuck instead on disenchantment. When the mind sees the drawbacks of ill will and thinks instead in terms of good will and forgiveness, that's how you destroy ill will. When you see the drawbacks of harmfulness, you think or act in ways that aren't harmful. All of these things are called meritorious fabrications *(puññābhisaṅkhāra)*.

When the mind fabricates these things, whether meritorious or demeritorious, it puts itself into a turmoil. Skillful thoughts have to keep working at doing away with unskillful thoughts. If you think too much, it can make you tired, both in body and mind. When this happens, you have to focus on a single preoccupation to bring the mind to concentration.

When you focus in concentration, throwing away both meritorious and demeritorious fabrications, and instead stay continuously stopped in a single preoccupation, this falls into the characteristics of imperturbable fabrication *(aneñjābhisaṅkhāra)*.

The sense of being snugly still or equanimous for long periods of time may not fit into the definition of imperturbable fabrications as *jhāna* or the higher absorptions. It's simply a type of immovability endowed with mindfulness and discernment. The mind is aware of itself, focuses its gaze right on itself, and knows itself continuously, without fabricating thoughts of good or evil. But this, too, can be included under imperturbable fabrication.

For that reason we have to find the aspect of the mind that can maintain its stance so as to see further in, so that it's not stuck on imperturbable fabrication. We have to penetrate to the point where we can see clearly in terms of the arising, remaining, and passing away, the inconstancy, stress, and not-selfness that are gathered in here as well.

You have to sharpen this basic principle of knowing so that it's razor sharp—so that you can see the truth that nothing has any true essence, that it's all illusory.

"Knowing" and "not knowing" trade places so that they seem to be different, *but if you get stuck on this duality, you're stuck on yourself.*

If you're really going to know, you have to know both sides: the side that knows and the side that doesn't know, to see that they're both inconstant in the same way, both deceptive in the same way.

Your sense of physical and mental phenomena is all fabrication. Mindfulness is a fabrication. Discernment is a fabrication. Even the still mind is a fabrication. When it's not still, it's a fabrication. So look at fabrication deeply, precisely, from all angles, inside and out.

Knowledge—even the observer, the knower—is also fabrication. They're all fabrications, whether they're right or wrong, good or bad. So you have to acquaint yourself thoroughly with fabrication. When you know fabrication thoroughly, in a way that penetrates deeply, it gives rise to a sense of disenchantment. If you don't do this, you'll hold on to the good fabrications and push the bad ones away.

We can recognize fabrications in that they change and disband. And then we realize that we've been playing around with these fake, imitation things all along.

Even clear knowing is a fabrication. It changes in line with physical and mental conditions. Mindfulness, discernment, and intuitive knowing-and-seeing are all fabrications—it's just that they're good fabrications, and we have to depend on them for the time being.

We have to understand fabrications, understand how to use them in a correct way, and then simply let them go. We don't have to keep holding on to them.

Knowing is a fabrication. Not knowing is a fabrication. When we examine them internally we see that both arise and pass away. Even the truths we know in this way don't stay long. They always turn into not knowing.

From this we can see that fabrications play all sorts of tricks on many, many levels, and we get deluded into playing along with them.

When we can get to know the tricks of fabrication of every sort on every level, that will be really beneficial. We'll really know in line with what the Buddha said: "*Sabbe saṅkhārā aniccāti*—all fabrications are inconstant." This is an important principle that will enable us to see through to the stressfulness in every sort of fabrication.

Even good fabrications, like mindfulness and discernment, are stressful in and of themselves because they have to keep changing. They're like tools we use for the time being, but we shouldn't stay fixated on them.

Even though we have to look after the foundation of our knowing, using mindfulness and discernment to supervise the mind, we should understand that the mind is a form of fabrication. Mindfulness and discernment are fabrications. If we know only on a superficial level and go around talking about what we've been able to let go of in our practice, we haven't seen deeply into fabrication. When this is the case, we still lie in the swirling currents of fabrication.

Correct knowledge, which is fabrication of a good sort, has to be trained to read and decipher things within and without, including itself, on many convoluted levels.

Once you've seen inconstancy and stress, you have to see through to the lack of self in fabrications of every sort.

You have to know that fabrication is inconstant, stressful, and has no self to itself. Keep looking at this again and again until it becomes clear to the heart. Only then will you develop a sense of disenchantment and dispassion. You won't fasten onto good fabrications or push bad ones away, for you've seen that they have the same price and are both equally changeable.

Even though we maintain the stance of our knowing, making sure that the mind doesn't fabricate even more, still we don't stay fastened onto the knowing, for it too has to change.

There come times when we think we know the truth in this matter, but then at later times or later moments even clearer knowing arises. That enables us to know that what we thought was true knowing actually wasn't. This knowing can change. No matter how much higher it goes as it changes, you have to remember that it's still fabrication; it can still change no matter what level it is. Whether it's crude or refined, you have to know it thoroughly. Otherwise you'll stay fastened to it.

If you can look in a way that sees all fabrications thoroughly—good, bad, right, wrong, the "knower," the "not-knower"—simply as the same sort of thing, your knowledge will gradually rise above these things. But even though it's above, it's still fabrication. It hasn't yet gained release from fabrication. Even the path is a form of fabrication. So when we develop the path, when we develop the factor of right view, we have to see rightly into this matter, seeing clearly into fabrication of every sort, no matter what the characteristics of our knowing. Whether we look at physical phenomena or mental phenomena arising and passing away, they're all fabrications. Even the mind firmly established in concentration is a form of fabrication, as are the stages of *jhāna*.

If we don't look inward, we make the mind dark and murky. Then when sensory contact comes, the mind can easily get all stirred up. So I ask that you make an effort to peer carefully inward to see what's there in the mind, to see how things arise, to see how mental labels and fabrications arise. That way you'll be able to disband them, destroy them, leaving the mind pure and simple, with no labels or attachments at all. It will then be empty of defilement. You might call it your inner beauty, "Miss Emptiness," who doesn't age, doesn't grow ill, doesn't die—a primal nature that doesn't change. This is something you have to touch right at the mind. It's not the mind itself, but the mind itself is what makes contact with it.

When we practice we're like diamond cutters. Our diamond—the mind—is embedded in dense, dark defilements. We have to use mindfulness and discernment—or virtue, concentration, and discernment—as our cutting tools to make the mind pure in all its thoughts, words, and deeds. Then we train the mind to grow still and to contemplate so as to give rise to clear knowledge. There you meet with what's totally pure and free from defilements and mental fermentations: our "Miss Emptiness," who is so extremely beautiful, free from change, whom the King of Death can't see.

And as to whether this is something worth aspiring to, I leave it up to you to decide.

APPENDIX

The following talks were given on the accompanying dates:

THE PRACTICE IN BRIEF	MARCH 17, 1954
AN HOUR'S MEDITATION	MARCH 3, 1977
A BASIC ORDER IN LIFE	JANUARY 29, 1964
CONTINUOUS PRACTICE	JANUARY 14, 1964
EVERY IN-AND-OUT BREATH	JANUARY 29, 1964
THE DETAILS OF PAIN	DECEMBER 28, 1972
AWARE RIGHT AT AWARENESS	NOVEMBER 3, 1975
THE PURE PRESENT	JUNE 3, 1964

GLOSSARY

Aggregate *(khandha)* Physical and mental components of sensory experience, which form the raw material for one's sense of self: form (the body, any physical phenomenon); feeling; perception; thought-fabrications; and sensory consciousness (counting the intellect as the sixth sense).

Anusaya Obsession, of which there are seven varieties: sensual passion, irritation, views, uncertainty, conceit, passion for becoming, and ignorance.

Arahant A person who has put an end to defilement and the mental fermentations, and thus is not destined for future rebirth.

Bodhisattva The Buddha prior to his Awakening.

Defilement *(kilesa)* Mental qualities that obscure the clarity of the mind. There are three basic sorts—passion, aversion, and delusion—but these can combine into a variety of forms. One standard list gives sixteen in all: greed, malevolence, anger, rancor, hypocrisy, arrogance, envy, miserliness, dishonesty, boastfulness, obstinacy, violence, pride, conceit, intoxication, and heedlessness.

Dhamma (Sanskrit: *dharma)* Dhamma with a small *d* (dhamma) means a phenomenon, an event, the way things are in and of themselves, their inherent qualities, the basic principles that underlie their behavior. Dhamma with a capital *D* (Dhamma) means principles of behavior that human beings ought to follow so as to fit in with the right natural order of things; qualities of mind they should develop so as to realize the inherent quality of the mind in and of itself. By extension, Dhamma is used also to refer to any doctrine that teaches about dhammas or Dhamma.

Establishing of Mindfulness *(satipaṭṭhāna)* The practice of using mindfulness and alertness to contemplate body, feelings, mind, and mental qualities as they are experienced in and of themselves.

Fermentation *(āsava)* Four qualities—sensuality, becoming, views, and ignorance—that flow out of the mind and create the flood of the round of death and rebirth.

Jhāna Mental absorption; a strong, stable state of concentration based either on a physical phenomenon or a refined formless dimension of the mind.

Kamma (Sanskrit: *karma)* Intentional acts in thought, word, and deed that result in becoming and birth.

Māra Death and temptation personified.

Name and form *(nāma-rūpa)* Physical and mental phenomena. Form is identical with the first aggregate (see above). Name covers the remaining four.

Nibbāna (Sanskrit: *nirvāṇa*) Unbinding; the liberation of the mind from mental fermentation, defilements, and the fetters that bind it to the round of rebirth. As this term is used to refer also to the extinguishing of fire, it carries the connotations of stilling, cooling, and peace. (According to the physics taught at the time of the Buddha, a burning fire seizes or adheres to its fuel; when extinguished, it is unbound.)

Noble Truths *(ariya-sacca)* The four categories for viewing experience in such a way that one can attain Awakening—stress *(dukkha)*, its cause, its cessation, and the path of practice to its cessation.

Paccattaṁ Individual, personal.

Saṅyojana Fetter. The ten fetters binding the mind to repeated birth and death are self-identity views, uncertainty, grasping at precepts and practices, sensual passion, irritation, passion for form, passion for formlessness, conceit, restlessness, and ignorance. The first three fetters are abandoned at the first level of Awakening, called stream-entry; the next two are abandoned at the third level of Awakening, called nonreturning; and the remaining five are abandoned at the fourth and final level of Awakening, arahantship.

Soḷasa Pañhā The Sixteen Questions, the final chapter in the Sutta Nipāta, in which sixteen young Brahmans question the Buddha on subtle points of the doctrine. Mogharāja's Question, mentioned in the talk, "All Things Are Unworthy of Attachment," is the fifteenth question.

Upakkilesa Corruption. A synonym for defilement.

Upāsikā A female lay follower of the Buddha.

INDEX

A

absorption. *See* mental absorption *(jhāna)*

addictions, 87–88, 115, 136

aggregate *(khandha)*, 239
    See also five aggregates

anger, 31, 43, 216

anusaya. See obsession

apt attention, 132

arahants, 19, 34, 59, 177, 227, 239

arising and disbanding
    contemplation of, 30–31, 221
    Dhamma as phenomenon of, 24
    in the mind, 10, 28–29
    natural phenomenon of, 166–67
    of perceptions, 29
    of phenomena, 2, 10, 169
    of sensations, 31
    truths of, 21, 25

ariya-sacca. See Noble Truths

attachment
    to the body, 1–2, 9–10, 90, 114,
      168–69, 180–82, 202–3
    as cause of suffering, 17, 107, 112,
      151–52, 154–55
    and circle of rebirth, 14–15
    to defilements, 40
    freedom from, 67, 83, 222
    letting go of, 106–23, 191, 220
    meaning and, 156
    by the mind, 103–5, 124–26,
      129–33, 164–65, 168–70, 209
    to sensations, 97–98
    and sense of self, 59, 105, 192, 205

aversion, 68, 82, 113

avijjā. See ignorance

B

Awakening
    gained by arahants, 227
    insights and, 173
    instants of, 160
    levels of, 241
    path to, 59

awareness
    See also mindfulness
    of breathing, 11–12
    eliminates suffering and defile-
      ment, 35
    within the heart, 22
    illusions within, 184
    inner, 37–38, 41
    maintaining, 19–29, 104–5, 123–39
    of the mind, 5–6, 13, 153
    of pain, 153–54
    pure and simple, 204–5, 224–26
    right, 211

B

becoming, 225

birth, 14, 106, 118, 120, 148, 160, 169
    See also rebirth

boastfulness. *See* pride

bodhisattva, 198, 239

body (form) *(rūpa)*
    See also five aggregates; self
    attachment to, 9–10, 90, 114,
      168–69, 180–82, 202–3
    elements of, 1, 168–69, 180–81,
      196–97, 202
    is inconstant, 30, 53, 127
    as a level of existence, 120
    and mind are the basis of existence,
      68

T
temptation, 15, 17, 87, 136
    See also Māra
tetrads, 51–53, 200
thought-fabrications
    caused by labeling, 31
    consciousness and, 155
    cycle of rebirth and, 166
    deceptions of, 164, 167
    as desire for illusions, 86
    elimination of, 125
    focusing on, 30, 219
    as a mental phenomenon, 2
    of the mind, 96–97
    perceptions and, 29
training
    to be mindful, 11, 178
    in breath meditation, 49
    of the mind, 5, 12, 33, 63, 78–79,
        163–68, 197–98, 198–200
    to see clearly with the mind, 2–3
    in virtue, concentration, and dis-
        cernment, 46
truth(s)
    See also Noble Truths
    of the body and mind, 14–15, 20,
        89–90, 121
    of the heart, 41
    of inconstancy, suffering, and not-
        self, 58, 73, 78, 170
    love of, 189
    of mental and physical phenom-
        ena, 21
    within/inside, 106, 112

U
Unbinding. See nibbāna
Unconditioned, the. See nibbāna
unfabricated phenomenon, 134, 228
upakkilesa. See corruption
upāsikā (female lay follower of
    Buddha), 241

V
vimokkha (liberation), 67
virtue
    See also precepts
    destruction of by pride, 122
    greed and, 190
    level of, 192
    purity in, 130–31
    of restraining the senses (indriya-
        saṁvara-sīla), 98–99
    as a tool to fight defilements,
        45–46
void, the, 185–86

W
wanting. See craving
water element, 1, 169
wind element, 1, 169, 196–97
wrong view, 210

FOOD FOR THE HEART
The Collected Teachings of Ajahn Chah
Foreword by Jack Kornfield
Introduction by Ajahn Amaro
416 pages, ISBN 0-86171-323-0, $18.95

"Ajahn Chah's wisdom, charisma, and simple teachings have had a profound effect upon the development of the Vipassana community in the West. Published on the tenth anniversary of his death, this collection brings together for the first time the Dhamma talks of Thailand's best-known meditation teacher and forest monastic, talks previously available only in rare or limited editions. It presents Ajahn Chah's teachings on meditation, liberation from suffering, calming the mind, enlightenment, and the 'living Dhamma'."
—*Tricycle: The Buddhist Review*

"In *Food for the Heart* we see a master at work. This is one of those books that can be opened to any page to find a wise teaching."—*Inquiring Mind*

"The talks in *Food for the Heart* cover a wide range of Dharma topics, and have been skillfully translated and edited to preserve the vibrancy, directness and humor that Ajahn Chah was known for. Though he taught for over thirty years, his talks were not systematically recorded and transcribed, which makes this collection from Wisdom all the more precious."—*Shambhala Sun*

"Ajahn Chah's teachings are simple, clear, and profoundly helpful. This book is a great contribution to the Dharma in the West."—Joseph Goldstein, author of *One Dharma*

"Ajahn Chah's words have the sharp sting, salty tang, and sand-dry wit of the old Zen masters. They will provide illumination and inspiration for all students of Buddhism."—Jan Chozen Bays Roshi, founding teacher at Great Vow Zen Monastery

"This rich collection is a real treasure. Profound, direct, earthy, and often funny, *Food for the Heart* will be especially precious for practitioners of Vipassana meditation in all Buddhist lineages."—Larry Rosenberg, author of *Breath by Breath*

"*Food for the Heart* will stand the test of time with the world's great classics of spiritual literature. An important volume for all serious followers of the Way."—John Daishin Buksbazen, author of *Zen Meditation in Plain English*

IN THE BUDDHA'S WORDS
An Anthology of Discourses from the Pali Canon
Edited and Introduced by Bhikkhu Bodhi
Foreword by the Dalai Lama
496 pages, ISBN 0-86171-491-1, $18.95

In the Buddha's Words is an anthology of the Buddha's teachings that has been compiled by a celebrated scholar and translator. For easy reference, the book is arranged into ten thematic sections ranging from "The Human Condition" to "Mastering the Mind" to "The Planes of Realization." Each section includes introductory essays and notes to help beginners and experts alike draw greater meaning from the Buddha's words. **Includes new translations, a glossary, and a foreword by the Dalai Lama.**

THE MIND AND THE WAY
Buddhist Reflections on Life
Ajahn Sumedho
228 pages, ISBN 0-86171-081-9, $16.95

"Wonderfully accessible and compassionate."
—Joseph Goldstein, author of *One Dharma*

"Sumedho's book deals with the nature of suffering and release from it by living a virtuous life awakening the mind to the impermanence of all things. He uses traditional insight meditation practices to open the heart and mind to the path of truth; he promotes a life of nonattachment, yet enriched with loving kindness; a simple life of nonexcess, profound goodness, cooperation rather than competition; and the mind that transcends but does not abandon the world. The keyword is balance. With its humorous observations upon his early days in Thailand, Sumedho's work is acutely practical and easy to read. Highly recommended for public libraries."—*Library Journal*

BEING NOBODY, GOING NOWHERE
Meditations on the Buddhist Path
Ayya Khema
Foreword by Zoketsu Norman Fischer
224 pages, ISBN 0-86171-316-8, $12.95

In this modern classic, Ayya Khema introduces the reader to the essence of the Buddhist path. She addresses the how and why of meditation, the nature of karma and rebirth, and the entirety of the Eightfold Path. With specific, practical advice, Ayya Khema illuminates the practices of compassion and sympathetic joy, and offers forthright guidance in working with the hindrances that we all encounter in meditation.

"A valuable guide to the path of meditative insight and loving compassion. It is direct, clear, and inspiring."—Sharon Salzberg, author of *Lovingkindness*

HEARTWOOD OF THE BODHI TREE
The Buddha's Teaching on Voidness
Buddhadhasa Bhikkhu
Foreword by Jack Kornfield
176 pages, ISBN 0-86171-035-5, $15.95

"In this remarkable book, Ajahn Buddhadasa teaches us beautifully, profoundly, and simply the meaning of *sunnata,* or voidness, which is a thread that links every great school of Buddhism. He teaches us the truth of this voidness with the same directness and simplicity with which he invites us into his forest."—from the foreword by Jack Kornfield

"One of the most prolific and influential teachers in our modern era. Wisdom does a wonderful service by publishing this precious taste of Buddhadasa's way."—*Turning Wheel*

ABOUT WISDOM

Wisdom Publications, a nonprofit publisher, is dedicated to making available authentic Buddhist works for the benefit of all. We publish translations of the sutras and tantras, commentaries and teachings of past and contemporary Buddhist masters, and original works by the world's leading Buddhist scholars. We publish our titles with the appreciation of Buddhism as a living philosophy and with the special commitment to preserve and transmit important works from all the major Buddhist traditions.

To learn more about Wisdom, or to browse books online, visit our website at wisdompubs.org. You may request a copy of our mail-order catalog online or by writing to:

Wisdom Publications

199 Elm Street

Somerville, Massachusetts 02144 USA

Telephone: (617) 776-7416

Fax: (617) 776-7841

Email: info@wisdompubs.org

www.wisdompubs.org

THE WISDOM TRUST

As a nonprofit publisher, Wisdom is dedicated to the publication of fine Dharma books for the benefit of all sentient beings and dependent upon the kindness and generosity of sponsors in order to do so. If you would like to make a donation to Wisdom, please do so through our Somerville office. If you would like to sponsor the publication of a book, please write or email us at the address above. Thank you.

Wisdom is a nonprofit, charitable 501(c)(3) organization affiliated with the Foundation for the Preservation of the Mahayana Tradition (FPMT).